Wrecked on the Feejees

by

William S. Cary

Double 9
BOOKS

Wrecked on the Feejees
by William S. Cary

ISBN: 978-93-69071-10-4

Published by

DOUBLE 9 BOOKS
2/13-B, Ansari Road
Daryaganj, New Delhi – 110002
info@double9books.com
www.double9books.com
Tel. 011-40042856

ABOUT THE AUTHOR

William S. Cary was an author and seafarer best known for his firsthand account of survival after being shipwrecked. In 1825, he was aboard the whaleship Oeno, which was wrecked on Turtle Island, part of the Fiji Islands. Cary was the sole survivor of the shipwreck, and his subsequent life among the Feejee Islanders became the basis for his memoir, Wrecked on the Feejees. The book details his harrowing experiences of survival, his encounters with the island's native tribes, and the complex relationships he navigated during his time stranded on the island. His narrative is one of resilience, as he describes the challenges he faced living in a foreign and often hostile environment, struggling to make sense of the cultural differences and hostile tensions with the islanders. His memoir stands as an important document of the-century maritime history and early American adventure writing. His remarkable survival story continues to captivate readers, reflecting themes of human endurance, adaptation, and the will to survive against all odds.

CONTENTS

FOREWORD

This thrilling tale was compiled from the log-book of William S. Cary, of Nantucket, the sole survivor of the crew of ship "Oeno", which was wrecked on Turtle Island, in the Pacific Ocean, on the 5th of April, 1825. It was first published in the Nantucket Journal in 1887, in installments, Cary's journal of his experiences having been discovered in one of the fish-houses below 'Sconset bank a few years before.

"The Wreck of the Oeno" is a personal description of the loss of a Nantucket whaleship, the capture and massacre of all but one of the crew, and the incidents of the life of the survivor among the cannibals of the South Sea Islands.

The ship "Oeno" was owned by Aaron Mitchell, of Nantucket, and was commanded by Capt. Samuel Riddell. She sailed from this island early in November, 1824, and as was usual in those days on account of the bar at the mouth of Nantucket harbor, went over to Edgartown to load for sea. The ship then proceeded, via the Cape of Good Hope, to the Bay of Islands. That was the last heard of her for nearly six years, and it was thought she had been lost at sea with all on board.

In 1830, however, the owner at Nantucket received a letter from William S. Cary, one of the crew, bringing the startling information that the ship had been lost on Turtle Island and that all of the crew had been massacred by the natives with the exception of himself, and that he was then living among the islanders.

The "Oeno's" crew consisted of Samuel Riddell, master; William Shaw, mate; — — Drew, second mate; three boatsteerers, a cooper, a carpenter, a cook, and a dozen foremast hands.

Cary's "log" of his experiences is a most graphic description of life among the Feejee Islanders. His capture and adoption by the king of the tribe, the life and customs of the natives, his escape and return home, are all touched upon in detail, the whole story forming one of the most thrilling tales of the sea ever printed. And the best part of the story is that it is true.

Harry B. Turner.

Nantucket, Mass., May 1, 1928.

CHAPTER I

The "Oeno" set sail at an early hour on the morning of November 4, 1824. The wind was light but fair and the weather pleasant. At 10 o'clock a. m. we discharged the pilot and got the ship snug for sea. As we neared the Gulf Stream the wind gradually increased, and on the afternoon of the 5th blew a gale from the northeast, accompanied by heavy squalls and rain. The ship was hove to under close-reefed maintopsail, and our green hands experienced for a season all the agonies of seasickness. The next day, however, the weather moderated and we made sail and proceeded with a fair wind.

We crossed the line on the 10th of December, and on the 16th sighted whales and captured three, which yielded 45 barrels of oil. On the 20th we sighted a large whale about half a mile ahead of the ship, and immediately lowered and fastened to him. He made 55 barrels. We proceeded on our course for the Cape of Good Hope, in doubling which we experienced considerable boisterous weather, and shaped our course for New Zealand. March 17th, 1825, we raised a school of whales and succeeded in taking four of them, which stowed down 50 barrels.

On the 20th we arrived at the Bay of Islands, where we found the ship Ann, of London, and bark Pocklington, of Sydney, N. S. W., the latter seven months out with 700 barrels of oil, and most of her crew sick with the scurvy. Nothing of note occurred here except that two of the crew, Henry Gordon and James Furse, deserted and we shipped two English sailors in their stead, and a native boy.

Having procured wood, water and vegetables, we set sail on the 7th of April in company with the ship Ann, bound home with 1800 barrels of oil. We intended to touch at Wallis' island, then proceed to the Kingsmill group to cruise for whales. We had strong trade winds, and on the 13th sighted and passed Pylstaat's island, one of the Friendly Islands. At sundown we shortened sail, by order of the captain who, on leaving the deck for the night, gave particular orders to the officers of the watches to have a good look-out kept and to call him immediately if anything unusual was seen.

In the middle watch (which was in charge of the second mate) between 2 and 3 o'clock a. m., the man at the helm saw white water and spoke to the second mate, who was sitting in the quarter boat, but he made no response. On seeing it again the man, who had at first supposed it to be a fish breaching, became satisfied that it was breakers, and sung out lustily to the officer, who sprang to the deck, but before a general alarm could be sounded, the ship struck on a coral reef. All hands were immediately called and the topsails clewed down. By this time the sea was making a clean breach over the vessel, and it was with the greatest difficulty that we could get about the decks, while nothing could be done to relieve the ship.

Mr. Drew, the second mate, immediately commenced clearing away his boat preparatory to leaving the vessel. The captain advised him to wait until daylight, but he persisted in leaving immediately and got clear of the ship with the boat's crew without accident, and pulled inside the reef into smooth water.

By the time daylight appeared every hope of saving the ship was abandoned. We got the starboard boat ready to lower and, watching a favorable opportunity, got clear of the vessel, narrowly escaping being swamped by a breaker which half filled the boat. We bailed her out and pulled into smooth water. Now two boats, with the captain, second mate and ten men, were safe, leaving the mate, William Shaw, and balance of the crew remaining on the ill-fated ship, which lay nearly upon her beam ends, with the sea continually breaking over her, and with only the weather boat in which to make their escape.

The boat was got ready, and the mate, stationing two men at the falls, picked the most favorable time and lowered down. The forward tackle was unhooked, and the boat's head swung around, but the after-tackle fall got foul and before it could be cleared, a huge breaker rolled the boat over, precipitating the crew into the water. At the same time the two men who had been stationed at the falls jumped overboard and all struck out towards the boats. We pulled up as near as prudent and rescued them all, though some were badly bruised, and one lad named Barzilla Swain had his arm broken by a cask before leaving the ship.

Though we were now all clear of the ship alive, it was with heavy hearts that we gazed back upon the wreck of what had so lately been our home. Land was in sight about three leagues off, and we headed towards it but soon found that a reef, forming a sort of hollow square about three miles long by two wide, enclosed us. We followed the reef around until we came to an opening through which we all safely passed. The water inside this reef was perfectly smooth and appeared deep.

Upon getting clear of the reef, we made the best of our way toward the land, and as we neared the shore, a man came down to the beach. We lay

on our oars and held a brief consultation, but decided it was better to land
and take our chances with the natives than to starve in our boats. Seeing us
hesitating, the man beckoned to us in a friendly manner to row along the
beach, which we did until we came opposite a landing. Seeing a number of
natives sitting in the grass and apparently making hostile demonstrations,
we again paused for consultation. The captain objected to landing at all and
proposed that we make the best of our way to Wallis' island, where there
was a chance of falling in with some homeward bound whaler. Mr. Shaw,
however, urged that the natives showed no signs of hostility, that what we
had taken to be clubs and spears were nothing more than sugar cane that
they had brought down to treat us with when we landed, and he argued
that we could remain here until the weather moderated sufficiently to get
what we wanted out of the ship to fit our boats, and then go where we liked.

Seeing our hesitation, the natives sent one of the oldest of their party
out in a small canoe. He paddled off until within a few feet of us but said
nothing. We had the New Zealand boy in our boat and the captain told him
to address the native in his language, which he did, but our visitor did not
understand him and soon returned to the shore. Supposing he was sent off
to invite us to land, we concluded to do so.

As soon as the boat touched the beach, Capt. Riddell jumped out, walked
up to the natives, and offered them his hand, but they took no notice of the
friendly greeting, and all rose and made for the boats. The captain told us
to let them take whatever there was in the boats, which was not much, as
he had everything thrown overboard that he thought would be valuable to
them for fear they might quarrel for the plunder and endanger our lives.
They assisted us to haul up our boats and gave us some of their provisions,
which consisted of sugar cane, coconuts, and a sweet root called mussarway
and was very pleasant to the taste. We offered them some of our bread, but
they would not eat it.

Some of the women came down to the landing, looked at us, and
returned to the town. Capt. Riddell took out his watch and placed it to the
ear of a native, who started back with fright and astonishment. He then
opened it and explained to them the use of it as well as he could by signs
and finally presented it to one of the chiefs, who appeared to be highly
pleased with it.

After their curiosity was satisfied, the chief said something to one of
the natives, who started for the town, making signs for us to follow, which
we did. After traveling nearly a mile over a rough stony path, we arrived at

the town, which consisted of about twenty houses. Two of these we found nicely prepared with mats, one for the officers, the other for the crew.

It appeared that there had been at some previous time more people on the island, as there were two villages of about twenty houses each, but only one was now occupied. The houses were built by setting posts in the ground, leaving them about six feet high and connected with rafters about twenty feet long. The roofs were thickly thatched with long grass, while the sides and ends were covered with reeds neatly bound on with rivets made from coconut husks. We found there were only about twenty-five inhabitants then on the island—some fifteen men and boys, the rest females. The men were large and well formed, of a dark color, some almost black. Their only covering was a strip of matting made from the bark of a tree twisted and wound several times around their bodies. The women wore about their waist a similar covering stained with different colors.

When we took possession of our new quarters it was about one o'clock p. m. The natives left us soon after and returned in the course of a couple of hours with baskets of cooked vegetables consisting of yams, tarrow packarlolo (a sort of pudding made of tarrow and coconut milk) and a kind of potatoes. They laid the food down at the door and repeated some words over it, then brought it in and made signs for us to eat, while they stood by watching us with interest, but not being very partial to our new diet, we soon finished the meal.

Several of us then started on a stroll about the island with some of the natives in search of water, which we found only in the hollow rocks, there being no pond or spring on the island; hence we were wholly dependent on the clouds for water, but we found coconuts, bananas, and a few bread fruit trees, also excellent fish in abundance.

We found we were on Turtle island, one of the Feejees, two miles long by one and a half wide, and surrounded by coral reefs. The island was broken and rocky but fertile and thickly wooded.

After our return the natives came and spent the evening with us, sung a song or two and evidently employed all their arts and powers of pleasing to reconcile us to our condition, and in return only wanted their curiosity gratified by watching our movements and examining our clothes and other things which we had brought on shore. When the natives left us we laid down on the mats and slept at intervals until daylight, when we mustered all hands to go off to the ship for clothing, provisions, etc., but we found that some of the natives were ahead of us.

Capt. Riddell started first in hopes to get firearms, but found the natives had secured them, and had loaded their canoes with whatever suited their fancy. They brought their plunder on shore and buried it. Our boats, which did not return till late in the afternoon, brought some clothes, bread, salt provisions and liquor, but found only one chest on board. What the natives did with the others we never knew. They continued their visits to the ship every day, taking out whatever suited their fancy. They could get off with canoes when it was not prudent to go with our boats. Some of us would frequently accompany them and pick up whatever we thought might be useful to us.

On the 15th, it being moderate, we went off and secured the spare boat, which was still uninjured. By this time we had nearly all out of the ship which would be of use to us, and seldom visited her. She had turned completely round, and begun to break up.

The natives were friendly and endeavored, by every kindness in their power, to make our situation as pleasant and comfortable as possible, furnishing us of their provisions in abundance, with which, and our ship provisions, we lived well. The natives generally spent their evenings with us and seemed to enjoy our company very much. Thus ten or eleven days passed without anything occurring to affect our pleasant relations with them. Capt. Riddell thought that after the full of the moon we should have moderate winds, and then we calculated to start for the Friendly Islands in our boats, which we intended to put an extra streak on, to better fit them for a sea voyage.

But the morning we had intended to commence operations, we were much alarmed by seeing a fleet of about twenty canoes approaching the island, with warlike demonstrations. Capt. Riddell went down to the beach and met the party, who were a frightful looking set, being hideously painted with red and black, and all armed with spears and clubs. The chief and Capt. Riddell walked up ahead, the rest of the party, numbering about eighty, following in single file.

They were all large sized men, many of them fully six feet tall. They wandered about the town a while, getting a good meal which the islanders had cooked for them. One of the party, apparently a young chief, sat down beside me and began talking, but finding none of us could understand him, he left us, seemingly much disappointed. The visitors showed no signs of hostility nor disposition to meddle with anything, but contented themselves with looking at us, and finally retired to their canoes for the night.

The next day they came to our house and seemed so friendly that our alarm quite wore off. Before leaving for the night, however, they were particular to ascertain our number. The following day they came up to town as usual, but there was a marked difference in their conduct. They began taking many liberties, which they knew would be offensive to us, and one of them came into our house, took some articles of clothing and was about making off with them when one of our crew took them away and helped him out of the house. This treatment he did not at all relish. He took his club and beat the ground most furiously, and expressed his displeasure by every possible gesture. One of our boys had on a red cap, which a native seized and made off with. The boy cried bitterly for the loss, when the fellow returned and gave it back. It seemed as though they were trying all ways in their power to provoke us to do something which would justify them in declaring war upon us. They were continually stealing everything they could lay their hands on, which made repeated quarrels with the least consideration of the crew.

Capt. Riddell took every opportunity to advise us not to use force and let them take everything they wanted, and gave his advice for our own good as well as his own, as we were without arms and wholly at the mercy of the savages. Well would it have been for the crew had they heeded the advice of our worthy captain. The inhabitants of the island continued to treat us kindly. They at one time brought us some yams. While we were eating them one of the visitors put his hand in the dish to take out a piece, when one of our crew rapped his knuckles, telling him to keep his black paws out of the victuals. This so enraged him that he went out of the house, got his club and beat the ground, using many threatening gestures. It is my belief that if the captain's advice had been strictly followed, and we had let them take whatever they chose without resistance, they would have left without molesting us. But through the inconsiderate conduct of such no doubt the lives of many valuable men were sacrificed.

The next day we made an ineffectual attempt to get to the ship, and on our return to the town we met a number of the savages who were the most troublesome, swinging their clubs as though preparing for battle. In the house where we lived all the spears and clubs belonging to the islanders were deposited. These they contrived to carry off, as they thought, unperceived by us. I was sitting in the house alone reading and observed the manoeuvers, which excited my fears, and I told my companions that I believed they would attack us that night. Some of them shared my apprehensions, others only laughed at my fears. The officers were fully satisfied of their design, but could do nothing to avoid it. That night I decided not to remain in the house, but went into the woods and slept in a cave. The night passed, however, with no hostile demonstration.

The next day Capt. Riddell, Mr. Shaw, Mr. Drew, myself and two or three of the crew were assembled in a look-out house on top of a rock, when one of the islanders came in with a most sorrowful countenance, as though he had something dreadful to communicate, looked at us a few moments, and then left without saying a word. I have no doubt but he came to warn us of what was going to be done, but that his heart failed him. The previous morning one of the islanders brought to our house in the valley six or seven spears and threw them in. It appeared as though they wished to aid us all in their power.

Soon after this kind savage left us, we heard a great shout in the valley below. The captain started to his feet in alarm and hurried out of the house, the rest of us following him. When we got down off the rock all but myself took the path that led to the town. I took a by-path that led across the island, well knowing what was going on in the town. A Sandwich Island boy followed me a short distance, then turned back. When I started I left Capt. Riddell standing at the foot of the rock. Which way he went I never knew. We parted, never to meet again.

CHAPTER II

I continued on this path, sometimes running as fast as I could, then I would stop not knowing where it led, and every moment expecting to encounter a native, until at length I reached the beach on the opposite side of the island. I followed along the shore until I came to a rock upon which I climbed, but could find no place of concealment so got down, and continued on until I came to another. This I climbed and on the top I found an opening leading into a large cave, which I entered and crawled into a crevice, not daring to go far from the mouth of the cave as it was so dark I could not see where it led. I threw down a stone and it sounded as though it fell forty or fifty feet.

The crevice in which I stowed myself was just big enough to admit me, and about ten or twelve feet from the mouth of the cave. During the night I heard the natives talking and heard their spears dragging over the rock. I had no doubt but that they were in search of me, so I kept very quiet, hardly allowing myself to breathe. I scarcely entertained a hope for life, well knowing that if I left the cave the natives would kill me, and if I stayed I should eventually starve.

Here I lay some six or seven hours endeavoring to decide upon some course of action, but without doing so I fell asleep, and slept at intervals until daylight. I then crawled out very cautiously upon the rock, being anxious to ascertain what had become of the crew. I thought it possible that the lives of some of them might be spared. I climbed a tree, to see if I could discover anything of the natives, but there were none in sight, so I ventured to walk along the beach until I came to the landing. The boat was there, but from the appearances I concluded the crew had all been killed, as there were many tracks in the sand and the beach was broken up and had evidently been the scene of a severe scuffle. I searched around until I found a place which had evidently been dug over. I scooped away a few inches of sand with my hand and came to the face of a man. I uncovered one other, but could go no further.

Sick at heart and almost famished, I started back toward my hiding place, scarcely knowing which way I went or what to do. I found a few raisins in the boat, which I ate as I went along. These, with a green coconut which I got in the morning and drank the milk of, was all I had eaten for two days, but was just enough to make me determined to live as long as I could and keep out of sight of the savages. I had now abandoned all hope that there was any of our crew left. Sometimes I would think I might as well give myself up to the natives as to remain in the cave and starve, for there was nothing that I could get to eat or drink, without great risk of being discovered, which I considered certain death.

On the third day I decided that I could stand it no longer and keep strength enough to be able to climb out of my cave, so I crawled out on the rock, took a look around, and as I did not see anything, I thought I would venture down to the shore and bathe. When I reached the shore I saw a party of women off fishing, near the reef. They soon discovered me and immediately started for the town, and I returned to my cave. I had not been there long when I heard voices. I looked out and saw two men evidently in search of me. I felt extremely loath to give myself up to be butchered, but my determination to live had been very much weakened, so intense had become my sufferings from hunger and thirst.

After looking at them awhile I decided to come out and end the suspense, so I crawled out in sight. They immediately started for me, one armed with a boat hatchet, the other with a knife. I sat down in the path with my back towards them, expecting to have the hatchet driven into my head, and not wishing to see the blow. They walked up until within a few feet of me, then stopped and looked at me a moment before they spoke. It seemed an hour. I looked around when one of them, an old man, a resident of the island and one with whom I had previously been on very good terms, addressed me kindly and wished me to go to the town with them. I sprang up and followed with alacrity, almost forgetting my thirst, but after we got off the rock, I made them understand I was very hungry and thirsty. We soon came to a coconut tree, when one of them procured a coconut, broke it, and gave me to drink, which greatly refreshed me. After we got to the town, the old man, who was a chief, carried me to his house and gave me as much fish and vegetables as I wanted. At dark he led me to a small hut in the woods where we spent the night.

The next morning we went back to the town to get some breakfast. We had not been in the house long when about twenty of our visitors came in, seated themselves, and began questioning me by signs to know if there were any axes or tools of any kind on board the ship. I told them I believed there were, thinking it might draw their attention from me. They remained awhile in animated conversation of which I concluded I was the subject, then left me in care of the old chief's wife, and went to the landing, launched their canoes, and started for the ship. They had not been gone long when another gang came toward the house. My old mistress on hearing them, said something, beckoned me to get behind her, which I did. They came up to the house, asked some questions and took their leave, much to my relief. But they had not done with me yet.

Late in the afternoon the savages returned from the ship, after an unsuccessful search for tools. They mustered all their party together in the lower town, and sent up one of their number after me. He came to the house and ordered me to follow him. On my showing some reluctance to obey, he seized me in no gentle manner and shoved me out of the house, so I put the best face on and followed him down to the town, or rather he followed me, keeping me ahead of him in the path.

When we came to the town I was horrified to see the savages all painted and armed similar to what they were at their first landing, but looking much more frightful to me. They all stood in a circle, and seated me in the center on the ground. My old friendly chief was sitting a short distance from the circle repairing some of the rigging to his canoe, to all appearances wholly unconcerned as to what was to be done with me. One of them went to him and asked him some questions, which he answered without even raising his eyes from his work. This was repeated several times.

After about an hour spent in consultation, during which the chiefs of the party appeared perfectly cool, but the common people manifested considerable excitement, swinging their clubs and looking as though they would like to have a crack at me, they all left and went to their canoes.

The old chief immediately came to me and spoke kindly, but I could not understand a word he said. He made me understand, however, that I was now his son, and as such he treated me all the time I remained with him.

The next day our visitors left, much to our satisfaction. I say our, as the islanders were no more fond of their company than I was, and I believe as much regretted what had been done as if it had been part of their own tribe that had been killed. I several times endeavored to learn some particulars in regard to the massacre, but they did not wish to talk about it and would only say that they had nothing to do with it. I did not understand their language and could only learn from them what they were disposed to tell me by signs.

I stayed here about a week longer, treated with the greatest kindness, when one day two large canoes were seen coming toward the island, which filled the natives with alarm. They ran to the town, collected all the property which they had gotten out of the ship and buried it in the woods. Seeing I was frightened they told me the canoes were from Lahcameber, and were friendly to white men, and not at all like the Ono men (our other visitors).

They soon landed and came up to the town. One of them seized me by the arm, and directly another came and took me by the other arm. The last one was a native of the Friendly Islands and much lighter than the Feejees. They were both chiefs and after disputing some time as to who had the best right to me, the Friendly Islander relinquished his claim and, to my surprise, addressed me in English, bidding me good morning. I returned his friendly salutation, after which my new master introduced me to their head chief who, I learned, was his brother. This chief was also brother to the head chief of Lahcameber. His name was Toka and he was a very amiable man. He immediately took me with all my possessions under his protection and made me understand that if any of his men offered to molest or rob me, he would correct them.

After Toka had got through with me, the Friendly Islander inquired what ship it was that was lost on the reef, and what had become of the crew. I told him it was the ship Oeno of Nantucket, and that all of the crew but myself had been massacred by a party from Ono. He shook his head, saying they were very bad. He then asked if the islanders had any of the plunder out of the ship and if there were any muskets. I told him they had secreted their plunder on seeing the canoes, and that the chiefs of the island had what muskets the Ono people had not got away from them. He said his party would get the whole or destroy the town, and if the inhabitants offered any resistance they would kill them all.

The next morning they commenced abusing the poor islanders shamefully and made them bring forward all the plunder they had got from the ship. My new master was armed with a four-pronged spear. He gave me a musket and kept me close by his side. I thought at first from their movements that they would destroy the whole town, but after they had secured all the plunder from them they retired to their canoes and did not trouble them more.

My old master was very sorry to lose me but did not dare to say a word. I certainly felt a pang of regret at leaving him, as he had probably saved my life and had always treated me with the greatest kindness. The Tongataboo chief was anxious that I should stop with him and go to Tongataboo with him, telling me that there were many missionaries there and plenty of ships came there, but I preferred continuing with my new master. I found these people were collecting tribute for the chief of Lahcameber from the islands which were tributary.

The next morning we set sail from Turtle Island and steered for Ono, I being in the canoe with the chief, and arrived the following morning. The natives were expecting us, it being the time for their annual visit to collect tribute, and had large quantities of provisions cooked and all things prepared for their annual feast. All the inhabitants of the island seated themselves in a large circle leaving an opening through which our party passed to the center, each one carrying a bundle of tappah cloth, which I found was intended for a present in token of respect and friendship. When they got inside the ring our chief stood in the center with the rest of the party around him, each one having a spear in his hand. These they commenced brandishing in the air, accompanying their movements with sundry antics and gestures which at first alarmed me, thinking they were hostile demonstrations, but I soon perceived it was only a kind of dance which was always performed on such occasion.

At the conclusion of the dance they threw down their spears and cloth and retired to a house prepared for us, after which the natives divided our presents among the chiefs, each one taking a share according to his rank. When this was settled they brought us the provisions they had prepared and presented them with a great deal of ceremony, then left us to feast upon them, which we did with good appetites. We remained here some ten or twelve days receiving tribute, which consisted of tappah, sinnet, oil and mats, and sometimes a few whales' teeth, which is the most valuable article they have among them. By this time we had received all they had to give, so took our leave of them and proceeded to Lahcameber, stopping on our way at Turtle Island and several others.

On the third day we arrived at Lahcameber. The landing was thronged with natives of both sexes, who received us with great joy. I was dressed in the Feejee costume (that is, no dress at all—only a strip of cloth around my body). I was accompanied to the palace, which was about half a mile from the landing, by the multitude, who gazed at me with much curiosity. The king's residence was situated in the center of the town, with a large square in front of it, neatly fenced in with reeds. The houses were neatly built, similar to those at Turtle Island.

I was led into the palace and found the king entertaining a party, with a kind of drink called carver. I was presented to the king and a Friendly Island chief, who could talk some English, through whom the king inquired who I was and where I came from. I gave him the full particulars of the loss of the ship and the massacre of the crew. He then offered me a cup of carver, which I dared not refuse, although my stomach loathed it, and it was with much difficulty that I kept it down. This beverage is made from a root. It is first chewed by the natives. Each person except the chief takes a piece of the root and, after chewing it sufficiently, spits it into a wooden bowl. It is then mixed or kneaded with the hands, a little water added, and strained through the thin bark of the coconut tree, when it is ready for use. It is then poured into coconut shells and handed round, each one having a shell of his own. After drinking heartily of it, it leaves them in a kind of stupor, similar to the effect of opium. Disgusting as this beverage was to me at first, my repugnance gradually wore away and after a while I could drink it with as good a relish as I can now swallow a glass of beer, though as I look back it makes my stomach turn to think of it.

After our visitors departed, the king, with the aid of the Tongataboo chief, asked if my chief at home would send out an armed vessel to punish those savages who had killed the crew and I told him I thought he would. He then wanted to know if I could clean his muskets—he had seven which came out of the Oeno which were very rusty. I told him yes, so he brought me some tools and I took them to pieces, he watching me all the time with considerable interest. After I had cleaned them and put them together, he expressed his satisfaction as well as he could by signs, frequently repeating the word caloo, saying if I had not have been a spirit I would have shared the fate of the rest of the crew.

The king then requested me to fire them, which I did several times, loading and firing as fast as I could, which frightened them very much. They all fell at every discharge as though they had been shot. The king then invited me to eat with him. The food was brought in a dish made from the leaf of a coconut tree, and consisted of yams and tarrow. I was seated beside the king. One of his wives brought in a large earthern pot of boiled fish, and six female attendants were in readiness to wait on us. One sat by the king to feed him and another was appointed to feed me. I at first objected to being fed, but the king insisted on my conforming to his rules as I was his son and ought to do just as he did, so rather than displease him I submitted. The water in which the fish was boiled was dipped out in coconut shells which were held to our mouths to drink. The fish was then taken out in a wooden dish and divided equally. While eating, all present held a green leaf in their hands, as a token of respect to the king. When the repast was finished all clapped their hands, repeating the word Hamdoo, which means give thanks to the king. A basket of coconuts was then brought in and each one treated to a share of the milk. The men having finished, the women were allowed the fragments. The women are never allowed to eat with the men.

The next day, after walking around the town and satisfying my curiosity, the king asked me to accompany him shooting and I, of course, accepted. We were accompanied by three of the natives and shot a few wild pigeons and a number of sea fowl which we found in abundance. Having no clothes on I was badly sunburnt and had a very sore back for a long time. Sea fowl were very plentiful about the shores and fish of excellent quality abounded around the island. These were caught by the women mostly, who were very expert, but the men considered it beneath their dignity.

Preparations were now making for a grand feast. The king sent people out in all directions to collect and cook yams, tarrow and all kinds of vegetables, also pigs, fowl, etc. The natives brought provisions from all parts of the island and deposited them on one side of a square before the king's house and retired to the other side to await the performance which was about to take place by visitors from the Friendly and Navigator Islands. They collected provisions enough for two or three thousand people, and when several thousand spectators had assembled, the king, with me by his side, was seated on an eminence built of stone on one side of the square. After all was arranged the actors made their appearances in two parties and took their stations in the square about twenty-five or thirty feet apart. One of them then stepped out into the open square and, brandishing a coconut stalk in his hand, challenged anyone to come out and fight him. His challenge was promptly accepted by a young native from the same party and a smart fencing match ensued. At last one gave up and the conqueror was greeted with shouts of applause by the spectators. Two others then took their places and so the sport went on. After one party had their turn the other came on and fought with their fists muffled with tappah, which seemed to delight the spectators quite as much as the club fight. They frequently shouted Wooa venaka! Suka venaka! (Very well done. Thank you, sirs!) After about two hours of this exercise one of them used some unfair play, which so enraged all parties that they flew to their clubs and spears, and I expected to see something besides a sham fight; but the king jumped from his throne, rushed into the midst of them and quelled the disturbance. They then seated themselves and the provisions were shared amongst them. After feasting they left us, some badly bruised and many with broken limbs.

When all had become quiet the king and myself, accompanied by his life guard and servants, went to a pond of fresh water to bathe. When the king leaves his palace he is always accompanied by his guard who goes ahead to inform all whom they may meet of his approach, as all are required to bow down until he has passed. They pay great respect to the king, whom they reverence as a superior being guarded by the spirits of his forefathers. This they are caught by the priests, called Umbaty, whom the king always consults before undertaking a voyage or any enterprise. The old priest (for they are always very old) commences shaking himself until every part of his body is in motion, pretending meanwhile to be talking to the spirits. He then takes a stalk with two or three coconuts on it brought to him by the king and beats it on the mats. If the fruit comes off easily it is a good omen, but if not the king postpones his undertaking till a more favorable time. After the Umbaty gets through with his ceremony he takes a drink of sea water which stops his shaking and drives the spirits out of the house.

While I was on this island we were visited by a party of chiefs from Ambow, bringing with them six or seven Manila men—mutineers from a Manila brig. They had killed the captain and officers and given themselves up to the natives at Ambow. I inquired if there were any Europeans in the brig. They told me there were three. One came from the Ladrone Islands and left the vessel before the mutiny. The others acted as interpreters for the captain and came near sharing his fate, but were protected by some of the crew who were not so bad as the ringleaders.

During their stay the king kept me close by him for fear they would entice me away. I was very anxious to go, but the king told me he was going to Ambow in a few days and I should go with him. The visitors came to invite us to go to a great feast which was preparing at Ambow, and in a few days they returned home in their canoes.

We now commenced preparations for our voyage. Messengers were dispatched to every part of the island to inform the different chiefs that the king was going to Ambow, and that they must send all the coconut oil, tappah, and whales' teeth they could produce for presents to the king of Ambow. Twenty large canoes were fitted for the voyage, and when all was ready the king went down to the squadron escorted by a large party of chiefs and subjects, five of his wives bringing up the rear and bearing with them the mats to sleep on and cooking utensils. We set sail with a fine breeze, made our passage through the reef which surrounds the islands, into the open ocean, and steered for the island of Emwaller, where we arrived about sunset and anchored near the shore. The king and myself slept on the shore. The inhabitants brought down yams, tarrow, pacalcolo and pigs which were divided among the occupants of the canoes, a separate share being set aside for the king and myself. The pig being rare done we built a fire, broiled it, and made a very hearty meal. The next morning we got under way and steered for the island of Engow, where we arrived, with the aid of our paddles, before sunset and anchored as before, which was done by sticking an ironwood pole into the sand, and making fast a rope with a running bowline that it might slip down to the bottom. Where the bottom is rocky they dive down and make the end of the rope fast to a rock or piece of coral. Here we received the same friendly treatment as at the other island, and the next morning steered for the island of Motosick, where we arrived in the afternoon. This island is about fifteen miles from Ambow.

Soon after our arrival here I saw a canoe coming from Ambow, in which was a white man. As they came alongside our canoe the white man reached out his hand and addressed me by name. I was dumb with astonishment. At last he said, "don't you know David Whippey?" "Yes," I answered, "I formerly knew him. He was a townsman of mine and an old playmate." "Well," said he, "I am that David Whippey."

CHAPTER III

My joy at this unexpected meeting was unbounded. It was now about a year since I had seen a white man. David inquired how I came there and I briefly told him my story. He said he had seen casks and pieces of boats which he had called American, and concluded that a ship had been wrecked on some of the weather islands. In his turn he told me his story. He had left the brig Calder some thirteen months before, bearing presents from the captain to the king of Ambow, together with a request that he collect all the turtle shell he could, the captain promising to return in a few months and trade with him for it. But now the time was so long that he had given up all hope of seeing the brig again. In fact, he had no desire to leave the island, as he was a particular favorite with the king and chiefs and was a chief himself. He informed me that there were two other white men who lived with him; one came in the Manila brig, the other had lived at the Feejees ten or twelve years. The king of Ambow valued the white men highly, as they had previously been troubled very much by the mountaineers coming down and committing depredations on the sea-coast villages. They were very much afraid of the white men's muskets, however, and had not troubled them since they had been with them.

It being near night and David's chief being anxious to get to the island of Ovalau, about seven miles distant, he took leave of me, expecting to meet me again at Ambow. We then landed and hauled up our canoes as our king had received intelligence that the king of Ambow was not quite ready for us, having to repair some houses for our reception, which had been partially burned a short time before. The inhabitants of this island brought us provisions in abundance, of which we ate heartily and then retired for the night. We spent three days here, and on the fourth launched our canoes and made sail for Ambow, where we arrived about ten o'clock in the forenoon and anchored, when the natives painted themselves, dressed and tied large bundles of tappah on their backs, as presents for the king.

When all was prepared we cast off and headed for the landing. When within speaking distance the natives saluted each other by shouting "Dohoah". (This word is used only to kings and chiefs.) Directly the queens came down to welcome our queens and escort them to the house prepared for their reception. They were very tastefully ornamented with most beautiful and fragrant flowers, and formed a line at the water's edge, repeating the word "myinafuandooa", which is the salutation for the queens. We then landed and proceeded to the house prepared for us, the king and his chiefs taking with them the loads of presents which, after some ceremony, were presented to the king.

The next morning I met David Whippey again, who came to invite me to the island on which he lived (Ovalau). We passed the day and evening very agreeably at my king's house. The chiefs, hearing of my intended visit with David, desired me to return as soon as possible. They had become very much attached to me and desired to have me in sight always, yet their kindly feeling toward me would not let them refuse me any liberty I wanted. I had always made it a rule never to oppose them and thus had got their perfect good will. The natural disposition of these natives is good and they possess kind feelings for those whom they like; they also possess strong passions and when enraged are savage beyond description and would kill anyone who displeased them with as little compunction as civilized people would kill a rat.

David spent the night with me and the next morning we started for Ovalau. This island was very much like the rest of the group, mountainous, well wooded, with plenty of water. A considerable portion was under cultivation. It also abounded with beautiful flowers of the most exquisite fragrance and all kinds of tropical fruits grew in profusion. The natives seemed very friendly. Here I spent three days very pleasantly and then returned to Ambow to my king, who was delighted to think I had come back so soon, but when I told him that I was going to stop with the king of Ambow, he was exceedingly sorrowful and used every argument he could to induce me to return to him. I told him, however, that I was anxious to get home and I thought my chances here would be better than at his island. He still insisted that I had better go home with him, and so it proved, for there was a ship touched at his island shortly after his return. Though he had the power to force me to go with him, he would not compel me to return against my will, and when I bade him good-bye he took me by the hand and said: "William, I am very sorry you are going to leave me. I shall be very lonesome when I go home without you, but I shall always be your friend and you will know where to find me." So we parted.

I then went to the king of Ambow and told him I intended to stop with him, which pleased him very much. He said he was father to all white people who came to stop with him, and so long as I was under his protection no one would dare molest me. He told me "Charlie" stopped a great many years with him, was a great warrior and conquered all the islands. I inquired of some of the white men who Charlie was and found that he was a white man who was cast away in the brig Eliza, of Providence, on the island of Nivy, about fifty miles northeast of Ambow. The rest of the brig's crew were taken off, but Charlie preferred stopping among the natives and came to Ambow, bringing with him three or four muskets and all the ammunition he could procure. When he arrived at Ambow he was a great wonder to the natives, being the first white man they had ever seen. The women and children were very much afraid of him and thousands of the inhabitants came to view him.

He had not been here long before war was declared against one of the neighboring towns, and an army was raised to go against them. Charlie applied to the king for permission to go with them and use his muskets, and after much persuasion was allowed to do so. When the attack commenced Charlie singled out one of the enemy's chiefs and, as he raised his spear to dart, he levelled at him and shot him dead. The natives, hearing the report of the musket and seeing their chief fall, immediately fled in the greatest confusion, the Ambow people following and killing all who came within their reach. They plundered the town, set fire to it, and marched home in triumph without the loss of a man. The king then made him head chief, giving him command of the whole tribe, and he conquered the entire group, but he was very severe with the natives and would shoot them for the most trivial offenses. Charlie was finally killed in a battle at the town of Uylah.

I remained at Ambow six or seven months and during this time made several excursions with them against their enemies to different parts of the island and to other islands. The inhabitants of the mountains and the sea coast are most always at war with each other. The mountaineers are very wild and savage, and often attack an unprotected town and massacre or make prisoners of all the inhabitants. The prisoners they eat. On one of these excursions to the island of Coroo, in one day we took and burned seven villages. We had to march over rocky mountains and through almost impassable woods. I was excessively fatigued. At night we had sentinels stationed round our encampment and the natives were drumming and singing most of the night, so that I slept but very little.

At daylight we continued our march through dense woods, over rocks and hills, until we arrived before the town of Angarmy, which we were going to attack. This was a large place and had a strong fence around it. Our army was composed of about 4,000 warriors, of whom about 100 had muskets. Before we commenced the attack our army was drawn up in a circle, and the head chief entered the circle with a bunch of reeds about ten inches long. Immediately all was silent. He gave a piece of reed to each tribe, and at the same time addressed a few words of encouragement, telling them that the town must be taken and each man must fight well and do his duty.

After this, one of the chiefs of each tribe ran towards him, holding his club over his head, saying: "This is the club for the enemy". After this ceremony they divided into parties so as to attack several places at once. As soon as we drew near enough the enemy attacked us with arrows and showers of stones. We then opened fire with the muskets, which frightened them so that they made offers of peace, offering all their whales' teeth and the chief's daughter, but their offers were declined, and when they found we were going to storm the town they fled to the woods. We entered the town and killed forty of the inhabitants. One man climbed a coconut tree to secrete himself. He was soon discovered and fired upon, but they did not kill him. The tree was then cut down by order of the chief, and the poor fellow was soon dispatched.

We then marched down to our canoes, taking with us five or six female prisoners and some of the dead bodies for a cannibal feast after we got home. The next morning we set sail and proceeded to Ovalau, where we stopped for the night, and the following noon arrived at Ambow. Before landing, all the young chiefs who had killed some of the enemy for the first time painted themselves red and black and each one had a staff with as many strips of white cloth fastened to the end as he had killed enemies. They then landed and marched up to the priest's house, where all the old chiefs and priests had assembled. They presented their staffs to the priests, who stuck them up near the house to remain as long as they lasted. The dead bodies were also carried before the priest and songs of victory sung over them, after which they were divided among each tribe.

In accordance with their custom, the young warriors did not enter any house for several days and nights for fear of offending the spirits. They believed that if they did not observe this ceremony they would be killed in the next battle. At night they formed a circle, marching round and round, singing and shouting, taking it watch and watch half at a time. After three or four days they washed off their paint and were at liberty to do as they pleased, believing then they would be protected by their gods in all future wars.

A short time after this we were visited by a tribe of natives from Raver, who came in two large double canoes, loaded with tarrow as a present for the king. These natives were the finest looking and most intelligent appearing of any I had ever seen. I took a fancy to go to their island with them and make a visit, so I asked the chief to carry me and he readily consented. I then went to the king and told him of my intended visit. He gave me liberty to go, but requested me to be sure to return. The next morning we started and soon arrived there, it being only about seven or eight miles from Ambow. I found it a most delightful place situated on the banks of a fine large river.

I was much pleased with the place and the people, and concluded to make it my home for a while, so I applied to a young chief (brother to the king) and told him I should like to stop with him. He seemed much pleased and told me to take the choice of his houses, of which he had three. I took one which was occupied by one of his wives (he had five) and lived here very comfortably, the chief's wife treating me with great kindness.

This chief had several brothers, all great warriors; the oldest was king, but the others wanted to be, so they got up a little conspiracy and declared war on him. He was too strong for them, however, so they made peace with him and went to Ambow. At this time all had been quiet for a year. One day, in company with a Manila man, I went down to a small island about three miles distant, fishing. We had rather indifferent luck and concluded to stop all night. Before morning news came to us that the king had been shot by one of his brothers who came from Ambow in a small canoe. It being a rainy, squally evening, he succeeded in reaching the town, unperceived, went to the king's house, pointed his musket through the doorway and shot him, wounding him so badly that he died in a short time. By the time the alarm could be given the assassin had fled beyond their reach. The Umbaty (priest) was called to save the king's life, but he was past his art and died sincerely lamented by his subjects.

The day after his death I attended his funeral. The chief was laid out on mats, with about one hundred fathoms of cloth wound around him. His face was painted black as though prepared for war, and his musket and war club lay by his side. His favorite wife sat at his head moaning most piteously and crying aloud, "Waloa nongu turang owsar cani lolocoo!" (Oh, my dear chief, I will soon follow you!) The rest of his wives, three more, came in and sat down beside the corpse and moaned bitterly—and well they might, for they were all to be strangled and buried with him. When all was ready, pieces of cloth were twisted up hard, a single turn taken around their necks, and a man took hold of each end. At a signal given by a chief (brother to one of the wives) these men hauled with all their might, and soon put an end to the troubles of the unfortunate women. They then kissed the hands and feet of the dead, carried them to the place appointed and interred them. The next day all the men and women shaved their heads, and the children had their little fingers cut off. This was done to show their sorrow and respect for the deceased. They believed that unless they did this the spirits of the dead would punish them by sending sickness and cutting off their crops.

CHAPTER IV

While I resided at Raver we went three months without rain, and the earth became parched and hard as a brick. The inhabitants were exceedingly alarmed at the duration of the drought. Such a time was never known by the oldest people. They expected to lose their crop of tarrow, which is a vegetable that grows only in very wet ground. It is very nutritious, and the natives are exceedingly fond of it. In fact, for months it is their chief article of diet. The chiefs went to the Umbaty a number of times to get him to intercede with their Caloo (God) to send them rain, but the old fellow's power did not reach the clouds. They finally concluded that it must be on account of the massacre of the Oeno's crew that they were so afflicted. I told them I thought quite likely that it was to punish them for killing white men. They said a ship was cast away at one of the islands some years before, and the crew massacred, and that immediately after there was a great sickness among them. They believed that the white man's Caloo was superior to theirs.

One night while at this island we had a severe earthquake. It had been a most beautiful evening, and I had been amusing the chief with stories of my country. Just before bed-time we went into the house, got out some yams and fish to eat and had just got seated when we heard a loud rumbling noise. The chief jumped and ran out of the house and before I could imagine what was the matter, the food was going one way and I another. I started to crawl to the door, fearing the house would be down on me, for by this time I perceived what the matter was, but before I reached the door it was all over. The next morning I asked the natives what was the occasion of the earthquake. They told me there was a monstrous great spirit, who lived on the big island in a very deep cave, whom they called Bookeegodinga. He laid on his back with his knees drawn up, and his least motion shook the earth, and when he rolled over, which was very seldom, it made a great earthquake. None of them had ever seen this giant spirit, but some had seen his cave. They frequently made him presents of mats, tappah and oil, carrying them to the mouth of the cave and leaving the Umbaty to get him to accept them. I presume he knew what became of them.

Shortly after this we visited the island of Cantab. We started in a large double canoe with about a hundred souls on board, and arrived about noon. The natives here showed the greatest respect to our chief, all sitting down on his approach, and remaining seated until he had passed. It is considered by them very disrespectful to stand when a great chief or king passes, or to talk loud on indifferent subjects in his presence, and it is sometimes punished with death. For such misdemeanor the offender must take an arrow or spear in his hand, and approaching the chief in the most humble manner, beg his pardon, and when the latter is satisfied that sufficient penitence has been shown, he grants his forgiveness. Sometimes for very great crimes, in addition to the above ceremony they are required to make liberal presents of whales' teeth. This is in cases of murder or for enticing away another man's wife, which is always visited with the heaviest punishment.

This island had formerly been under its own government. The natives were great warriors, and had never been conquered until the people at Raver got muskets and subjected them, making them tributary to Raver. The Raver natives considered them very valuable subjects. I heard there was a white man residing on the other side of the island and asked my chief for permission to visit him, but he refused saying it was an enemy's town and the Raver people dared not go there. The fact was, however, that he was afraid I should not come back. While here we were supplied by the natives with provisions in the greatest abundance. We remained a few days collecting tribute, and returned home deeply laden with tappah, mats and coconut oil, which was divided among the chiefs according to their rank.

The dialect of these people differed from any I had ever visited, but their manners and customs were the same. Cantab is a small but high island, about ten miles long by four wide. On the western end there is a mountain shaped like a sugar loaf, at the foot of which there are two springs, one hot or very warm, and the other nearly as cold as ice. I bathed in the warm one, and could but just endure the heat. Many of the natives had never beheld a white man before and eyed me with great curiosity, but I was not much troubled with the children, as they were very much afraid of me and if I looked toward them they would scamper off like sheep.

When at Raver, I used to employ myself fishing, shooting and doing little mechanical jobs for the chief. I used to have very fine shooting, there being vast numbers of ducks round the river. The natives were very expert at shooting them with arrows. One day I was in the house casting a lead pipe for the chief, when suddenly he called out "awanker parpalong sarla comy"! (The white man's vessel has come!) I inquired where and how he knew. I learned that a canoe was off near her and started to go on board, but seeing a smoke they were afraid she was going to fire guns, and dared not go, but immediately came ashore and reported. The chief ordered his canoe and we started down the river. When we got to the mouth of the river we found the ship lay about three miles from the reef, with the maintopsail aback, but the water was so shoal that we grounded on the reef, and before we could get over she braced full and stood off. My heart ached to see her go. This was the first ship I had seen for over two years. We returned to the shore and built large fires in hopes she would continue round the island till morning, but when day broke we could see nothing of her. The chief thought she had gone to the island of Cantab and some of our party proposed going there if I would accompany them, which I readily consented to do. We accordingly started in a small canoe, but when we got to the passage through the reef, we found the sea too rough to venture out, so we ran down inside the reef four or five miles to a small village where we procured a large canoe and crossed over to the island of Banger, about five miles distant. By this time it was near night with a strong wind and rough sea, so we concluded to stop there for the night. We secured our canoe and started for the village, which was at the summit of the highest mountain and about three miles from the shore. After a tedious walk over rocky hills and through thickly-wooded valleys we arrived at the village, reported to the chief and were assigned a house calculated for the accommodation of visitors, with which every village is provided.

Through the night the inhabitants were employed cooking pigs and vegetables, which were presented to us with the usual ceremony. The morning brought a severe storm of wind, rain, thunder and lightning. All we could do was to make ourselves comfortable. In the course of the day our chief sent for an old Umbaty who was celebrated for his knowledge of the future, and told him he wanted to know if there was a ship at Cantab or any of the neighboring islands, also when the storm would subside so that we could continue our voyage. The old man sat motionless for a few moments, then got up and left us. Directly he returned bearing in his hands a few green leaves. He sat down in the middle of the house, and rubbed the leaves until the juice began to run. He then held his hand with the juicy leaves straight up over his head and said: "If this juice runs down to my shoulder without dropping off she is there, but if not, she has gone some other cruise." He then squeezed the leaves and the juice ran down to his elbow and dropped off. "Ah!" he said, "she is not there." Other questions he answered the same way.

This island is much like the others, high and well wooded, and very fertile. The inhabitants were not so numerous as on other islands of the same size, owing no doubt to their continual wars. Our chief told me that till within a few years the natives here were very savage and if a canoe landed for shelter in a storm or in distress they would kill all hands and have a cannibal feast.

At sunset it cleared off and we proceeded on our voyage, arriving at Cantab the next morning, but could learn nothing of the ship. We then proceeded to Tarbuca where we concluded to make a stop. While here the chief requested us to assist him to capture a village, the people of which were very troublesome to him. We consented, mustered our forces and started one morning, but found the enemy prepared for us. We had two muskets. I had one and a chief another. We gave the war whoop, and advanced to the attack, firing our muskets and wounding two, whereupon they all fled, taking with them their wounded companions. Some of our men followed them and killed one chief, who they slung on a pole and brought back. They took the dead body to the square and sang songs of victory over it, then carried it away and had a cannibal feast. The following night one of the Tarbuca men went to this village and offered to join them. They readily accepted him. After telling them some fine stories he induced one of them to accompany him on the pretense of securing some plunder. He got him near the town, knocked him on the head, shouldered him and brought him into the town. For this act he was well rewarded by the chief. We started for Raver with our canoe loaded with presents given us for assisting in conquering the village, and arrived the same day, having been absent about a fortnight.

Some time after this I obtained permission to visit Ambow. My chief furnished me with a canoe and two men. We started in the morning and reached Ambow in the afternoon. I went direct to the king, who was delighted to see me and treated me to the best he had. He asked me if I had come back to stop with him, but I told him I should return the next morning, having only come to see him and inquire after his health. He seemed very much flattered that I should have manifested so much interest in him. I also went round and visited the chiefs of my acquaintance, who were exceedingly glad to see me, but all regretted that my visit was to be so short. The next morning we returned to Raver.

A short time after our return we were visited by a party from the big island called by the natives Vechalaboo, bringing with them presents of tappah and salt for the king of Raver. These presents were brought up to the public square, which is used for all grand occasions, and distributed with the usual ceremony. After this our chiefs had a dance by themselves. They formed in a straight line with the head chief in the center and the singers behind. When the singing began (one singing a line or sentence alone, then all repeating) the chiefs kept time with their hands and feet with great regularity. They had no music but singing, though when they went through the spear exercise, they made a kind of drum by resting the ends of a stick of timber some five feet long on blocks, and beating on the middle with sticks about the size of drum sticks.

I always had the privilege, at the time of receiving presents, of selecting whatever I chose, and generally availed myself of it. Sometimes when the natives thought I was helping myself rather too freely they would call out that a certain subject was tabooed, but I would tell them it wasn't tabooed for me to take what I liked. Salt was a scarce article among them and much valued. It was made in artificial ponds by the heat of the sun, and they brought all they had for market to Raver. The king of Raver had married the big island chief's daughter. From Raver the salt was carried to Ambow, and exchanged for tappah, oil, mats, etc., and from there it would get distributed over most of the islands. It was manufactured in large cakes—some of them as large as two men could carry on a pole. When our visitors departed their canoes were loaded with presents from our people consisting of mats, tappah, and oil scented with sandal wood and flowers.

This large island is separated from Raver by a channel only about a mile wide. It was thickly settled and its inhabitants were continually at war with each other. Indeed the principal occupation of the men, when not on the war path, was the manufacture of clubs, spears, bows and arrows, and other implements of war. Their dialect was so different from ours at Raver that I could understand very little they said. (As the reader may surmise, I had by this time quite mastered the language of the natives with whom I had resided.)

There were great numbers of green and hawk's bill turtles around the shores and an abundance of fish which they caught with their nets. They would spread their net in the form of a half moon outside the fish or turtles, secure it by sticking down poles, then drive the game towards it by splashing the water. When these islanders were preparing for a fishing cruise they were highly offended to be spoken to, and when addressed refused to answer, and if anyone stepped on their nets or fishing gear, they would postpone their cruise till another day. They believed that if they conversed with anyone at such times they would be eaten by sharks, or some other dire calamity would befall them.

It now being the planting season I went with the king one day to witness their operations. At planting time it is customary for the neighboring towns to join and assist each other. We went over the river to a town on the opposite bank, where we found all hands employed in breaking up soil and preparing it for the seed. This was done with a kind of shovel made from a large pearl shell with a handle or pole fixed to it. They dug up the earth and hove it up in heaps about four feet apart, each heap being calculated for a hill of yams. The king told me to select a piece of ground for myself, and he would have it dug, which I did. After the ground was thus prepared they returned to Raver and had a feast.

The next day the women went out and planted the yams. These were planted about the same as we plant potatoes. The large ones were cut into several pieces and the small ones planted whole. They put one or more in each of the heaps of earth, covered them lightly with soil, and then put a handful of white sand on each, that they might know when it was all done. At every planting season they plant a piece of ground for the Caloo (God). This is done principally by the chiefs, the women not being allowed to plant this for fear the Caloo will be offended and destroy their crops. The ground for the Caloo is dug up with an ironwood stake and made up in heaps about four feet high with their hands. They plant a hill on each heap and set a white flag on a pole at each hill, thinking that this will insure them a good crop. Tarrow keeps continually growing. They pull up a root and cut it off, then stick the top down and a new root grows. After the yams sprout they stick a reed in each hill for the vine to run up on. After this they are left to the care of the women, who keep them clear from weeds with a hoe made from a pearl shell.

The chiefs at Raver frequently employ themselves in making baskets, which they weave very neatly and handsomely from a kind of grass which they cure and dye various colors. These baskets are traded off to the other islands.

The most of the chiefs had muskets and many of them were excellent shots, but the common people seldom used one. It was very rare for them to have property enough to buy one and if they did, and the head chiefs or king took a fancy to it, they would take it away from them. They sometimes would want to fire my musket, and I generally let them, always putting in a heavy charge. They would hold the gun at arm's length, and when they fired she would jump out of their hands. This puzzled them very much. They could not understand why she did not jump when I fired her. I used to frequently accompany the king on his gunning excursions. He was an excellent shot, and prided himself very much on his skill, and was always highly elated when he beat me.

The island of Raver is about five or six miles long and only about two miles across in its widest part. It had five or six different villages, some of them small. The one where the king resided was much the largest, containing upwards of a hundred houses. Those occupied by the common people were very small, but those belonging to the king and chiefs were much larger.

The one occupied by the king was about forty feet by thirty wide. At each end he had a temporary floor across from the eaves forming a loft. These lofts he used to deposit his treasure in. One end, where he slept, was raised from the ground with dry grass covered with mats and a curtain drawn across to keep out the mosquitoes, which were exceedingly troublesome.

While I was here the king built a house for their Caloo Laboo (Great Spirit). This was perfectly round. The center of the roof went up to a very high peak, which was supported by a post in the ground. Across this peak a spar was fastened, which projected eight feet beyond the house, and was covered with small white shells, and a string of the same ten feet long was suspended from each end of the spar. This was built as an offering to the Great Spirit, who had given them power over their enemies, and was placed in charge of the Umbaty, who was supposed to frequently see and converse with the great Caloo.

They generally cook in the house, having the fire-place in the middle of the building. They used earthen vessels to cook in, made in the form of a jar. At one of the villages on this island they manufactured this kind of ware and their water jars were very handsomely glazed with the gum of a tree. This labor is all performed by the women. They bake it in a kiln. This ware forms an article of traffic for which they get tappah and oil from the other islands.

One morning the king sent a messenger to the king of Ambow. In the afternoon he returned with a letter to me from David Whippey, informing me that there had been a ship seen by the natives and that some of them had been on board and conversed with the captain, who could talk with them enough to inform them that he was going to Myambooa after sandalwood. He (David) wished me to come to his town and go with him in pursuit of the ship. I informed the king of the contents of my letter and promised him that if he would let me have a canoe and two men to go to Ambow and from there get to the ship, I would procure him a musket and some powder. He was much pleased and promised that he would have the canoe and men ready in the morning. I spent a sleepless night. The thought of once more getting on board a ship drove sleep entirely from my eyes.

CHAPTER V

Morning came at last and I found my chief as good as his word. The canoe and men were ready and I immediately embarked for Ambow. I found the old king there as glad to see me and as kind as ever. He told me the white man's vessel had come to one of the islands and inquired if I was going to find her. I told him that was what brought me to Ambow, and that I wanted him to furnish me a canoe to go over to Ovalau to find David, as he had sent for me to go with him. He accordingly procured me one from the fishing people and I was soon under way. The king told me I must come back and not go in the ship, but tell the captain to come and trade with him for beche de mer[1], all of which I readily promised.

When about three miles from Ambow the wind died out, and as night was coming on the natives refused to proceed, despite my entreaties, so we landed on a small island and spent the night. Next morning we got under way and arrived at Ovalau about noon. I found the white man who lived with David Whippey and he told me that David had gone to one of the neighboring islands, but would be back the next day and that he was waiting for me to go to the ship. The next day David returned, but as it was late in the afternoon we decided to wait until the following morning. It was now about a year since I had seen David and we spent the night very pleasantly.

Early in the morning the chief's double canoe was launched and prepared for the voyage. We made sail, having about twenty natives for crew and six of us passengers—three whites and three of the brig's crew who belonged to the island of Yap, one of the Caroline islands. (After the mutiny they attached themselves to David and had been with him ever since.) We ran this day about fifty miles N. E. and arrived before sunset at the island of Booyar, where we stopped at a small village tributary to Ovalau. Here we learned that the ship was at anchor at Myambooa bay and that the captain had been trading at the islands before. The natives brought us provisions as usual. They seemed to be a poor tribe. Their houses were small and poorly built.

We were detained here by head winds for three days, which to me seemed a month, so impatient was I to reach the ship and anxious lest she might leave before we could get there. On the fourth day the wind and weather were favorable and we started for Myambooa. As we neared the mouth of the bay we discovered a canoe steering for us, and supposing it to be enemy we immediately prepared for action. Our muskets were loaded and the natives bent their bows, but on their drawing near we saw it was an Ambow canoe that had been to the ship, and that she had a well-dressed white man and one of the Manila men on board.

The white man hailed us and inquired where we were from. We told him, and that we were in pursuit of a ship which we had heard was at Myambooa. He told us that it was the ship Clay, of Salem, Capt. Benjamin Vandaford, and that he was the second officer. He said they were on a trading voyage for sandalwood and beche de mer, and that he was now bound to Ambow, having heard of there being turtle shell and some dollars there. He inquired as to the truth of the report and we told him we knew of none, except what the king had in his possession. David offered to go back with him to assist in trading, and after some hesitation he took him. We then proceeded to the ship. I was invited on board and kindly received by the captain and his officers, and soon acquainted them with my story, and engaged passage in the ship to act as interpreter and assist in procuring a cargo.

This was in October, 1827. The next day the chief of the island visited us, bringing with him some sandalwood for a present to the captain. The captain wished me to tell him that he wanted a house built for curing beche de mer on the south side of the bay. The chief agreed to build the house, but advised having it on the other side of the bay, as there was not timber enough on the south side and it would take some time to transport it. The captain, however, insisted upon having it built on the south side, as it would be nearer the ship and more convenient landing. So he went on shore and selected the site, and the chief soon had the whole tribe at work cutting timber. The location of the house was such that it could be protected by the ship's guns in case of attack from the natives. The work progressed so fast that the house was soon ready. When the pots were set and everything prepared for curing the beche de mer, the captain sent me off to the reef with a boat's crew after the fish, which we found quite plenty and we soon returned with a boat-load. After breakfast they were landed and prepared for cooking and curing.

The method of doing this is as follows: The fish is cut open at the mouth and the entrails squeezed out. It is then boiled for half to three-quarters of an hour, then skimmed out and laid on a flake to drain. When sufficiently cool it is squeezed with the hands, put into baskets and carried to the drying house, where it is spread on flakes built over a trench, in which there is a slow fire. After remaining there twenty-four hours it is shifted to a flake above, where it remains two or three days. It is then put into bags and carried to the ship, where it is carefully picked over, and what is sufficiently cured is sewed up in bags, weighed, and stowed away ready for market.

The natives brought beche de mer in the greatest abundance—quite as much as we could take care of—and the prospect was very good for speedily procuring the desired supply. But one day, while we were on board at dinner, our house was discovered to be afire. The captain ordered two boats to be manned and armed, supposing it had been set on fire by the natives. On reaching the shore, however, we learned that it had caught by accident on the inside, and those in charge were unable to extinguish it. It burned to the ground and also consumed a considerable quantity of our beche de mer. That afternoon David arrived from Ambow, bringing a letter from Mr. Driver, the second mate, which stated that he had built a house and found the beche de mer very plenty. He had got about forty piculs (a weight of 133 1/3 pounds) cured, most of it of a superior quality. He had spent all his articles for trade and wanted more sent.

Upon receiving this intelligence the captain decided to go to Ambow with the ship and not attempt to rebuild here. So he collected what sandalwood he could, paid off the men he had employed, made the chief some presents and got under way. We beat up some five or six miles and came to anchor under the headland of Naviti, where we lay three days. We went on shore with the boat at the town of Naviti to trade for vegetables, etc., and loaded our boat with coconuts, bananas and sugar cane, for which we paid a few beads and trinkets. This island is one of the largest in the group and is laid down on the chart as "Thowcanrover".

Myambooa is the largest and most convenient harbor to be found at these islands. The south side of the bay is formed by a low, narrow point of land. The north side is very high land and there are several villages located there but none near the shore. The village of Myambooa is the principal place in this part of the island. It is situated near the entrance of the bay, but some distance inland, and a river runs past the village. While lying here in the Clay I went up this river with Captain Vandaford and found the water very shallow at the mouth, with a very crooked channel, but after getting over the bar found plenty of water. On each side of the river are large groves of mangrove trees, with their trunks below the surface of the water covered with oysters, some of which we tried and found very good.

Above these trees stood the village of Myambooa, which was a small place and the houses quite inferior. The natives depended upon their neighbors for mats and other domestic articles, for which they paid principally with powder and other articles which they got mostly from ships. Their location gave them much the advantage in ship trade, as it was the only place where sandalwood could be procured in any considerable amount. Captain Vandaford had made two or three voyages here before, found sandalwood plenty and bought it very cheap.

On the fourth day, the wind favoring us, we got under way and ran down to the island of Goro, where we shortened sail and hove to near the shore. The natives came off, bringing us yams and other provisions, which we bought with knives, beads, etc. The next morning we made sail, and proceeded to Ovalau, where we arrived in the afternoon, and anchored off the western side near the shore. After getting the ship snug a boat was sent to Mr. Driver, who was trading at the island of Bever, about two miles from Ambow and ten or eleven miles from the ship. When the boat returned we got under way and went nearer to the island where Mr. Driver was employed and came to about two miles from the shore surrounded with broken coral reefs. All hands were then employed rigging boarding nets and getting ready for trade.

We were soon surrounded by natives from Ambow and adjacent islands. The king and governor of Ambow came on board to inspect the ship, bringing with them a few trifles as presents to the captain. The ship's sides were thronged with natives, but none were admitted on board except those of high rank. To enforce this we had to keep men stationed around the ship to once in a while prick the natives off when they became too bold. After those on board had satisfied their curiosity, the captain directed me to tell them that he was going to Ambow and would like to have their company, to which they consented, so the boat was prepared for their reception, and we finally succeeded in getting them into it.

After we got off from the ship I told them, by the captain's order, that the ship would fire a salute in their honor, which she did, and they were highly delighted. On the way to the shore they commented freely on the ship, her construction and the grandeur of her appearance, and inquired how long it took to build such a noble vessel. They were perfectly astounded when I told them that one could be built and fitted for sea in three or four months. They could hardly credit it, since it took them three or four years to build a canoe. We soon landed at Ambow, where the natives were assembled in great numbers to see the captain. The king's house was the first place we visited. The inside was covered with new mats and everything arranged to show to the best advantage to the visitors. Captain Vandaford gave the king's wives a few small presents. We then took a stroll around the village and I pointed out to him the different chiefs' houses. On our return to the ship we found the natives, whom we left there, still viewing the different parts and objects about the ship with evident interest. They measured her length and breadth, and counted her masts over and over, counting the bowsprit as one. They called it spineringarselar.

The next day we went on shore to the beche de mer house and found the trading officer busy purchasing beche de mer, with which he was already over-stocked. We loaded our boat with the cured and returned to the ship. The natives were continually bringing fruit and vegetables, which we bought very reasonably. The king and his officers having had their visit, next came the queen and her retinue, to whom all requisite attention was paid. They were invited into the cabin. They were at first rather timid, fearing some evil was intended, but upon my assuring them that they would not be harmed they ventured down. They appeared delighted with the cabin furniture and indeed with everything they saw. The captain made them some trifling presents, but they thought as they were persons of the first rank he had ought to have given them more. One of them asked me why the captain was so stingy—said he was a great captain and ought to be liberal, but he wasn't like massa Raver (Mr. Driver) who gave them a great many presents and was the best white man that ever traded among them.

Mr. Driver on shore was continually crowded from morning till night with women and children bringing beche de mer, mats for bags, fruit, vegetables and everything which they thought he would buy. The price of a musket was sixteen hogsheads full of beche de mer, which it took them five or six days to get from the reefs. Some of it they got in two or three fathoms of water, diving for it, and bringing up one or two at a time. That obtained in deep water is the most valuable kind to the Chinese. When first taken it is about a foot in length and from three to four inches wide. The under side or belly is flat, and the back rounding. When taken it is quite soft, and if not boiled soon spoils. The entrails and water which comes from the fish is of a bright purple and those employed in opening them get their hands so stained that it is impossible to wash it off. It is quite lifeless. We never found anything inside but this purple water and coarse sand and gravel. The back is covered with prickles from an inch to an inch and a half in length. When taken it is of a reddish cast intermingled with white, but when properly cured is entirely black.

To procure it the natives go out on the reef, let the canoe drift, with their eyes fixed on the bottom, and when they see one, dive and secure it. When cured the prickles become hard and brittle as glass. Captain Vandaford took one of this kind on board and weighed it green. It weighed five pounds, but when cured it only weighed three quarters of a pound. There are five or six different kinds of beche de mer. One kind is about a foot long and three inches in diameter, smooth, and of a reddish black color. The mouth is very small and round and has four or five teeth. It is not as soft as the prickly kind but is generally found with it in deep water. The two kinds are scarce and hard to get, but are much more valuable than the kind we got at Myambooa, which were of the same form, but much smaller and black, being found in much greater abundance and more easily obtained, as it is found in shallow water.

After being here some time we experienced a heavy gale of wind from the southward. We put out three anchors and sent down our light spars. We were surrounded with reefs, one not more than a cable's length astern, but having good holding ground we rode out the gale without material damage. Many of the houses at Ambow were blown down. The gale lasted about twelve hours, then moderated and shifted to the northward, blowing as hard as before, but did not last long. When it abated we sent a boat ashore after beche de mer. Mr. Driver had all he could do during the gale to prevent the house from blowing down but by the aid of guys and shores had kept it up. Most of the thatch had blown off, however, and the house was flooded with water. He had led the water off by means of a ditch and was now ready for business again. When we had procured six or seven hundred piculs the captain thought it best to start for Manila, so as to get there before the change of the N. E. monsoon, so we broke up the establishment, paid off the natives, made the king and chiefs suitable presents and got underway for Ovalau where we arrived the same afternoon.

I then concluded to leave the ship. It was now the 17th of February, 1828. I wrote a few lines to the owner of the Oeno, informing him of her loss and the fate of the captain and crew, which I gave to Capt. Vandaford, informing him that I should remain at the islands till his return from Manila. David Whippey was on board, and we stopped for the night. The next day the ship got under way and stood clear of the land and backed her maintopsail.

The captain gave us (David and me) a boat into which he put a keg of powder and musket for each, besides several small articles. He requested us, if he got in any trouble or was in sight next morning, to come off, which we promised to do, and shoved off. The ship fired a gun and gave us three cheers, which we answered; she then squared away and stood on her course, and we made the best of our way ashore, arriving at the village of Labooca about sunset. David's chief was almost beside himself with joy when he found that he had not gone in the ship, but he had not the remotest idea of leaving.

After stopping a while with David I made a visit to Ambow. The king was surprised enough to see me, supposing I had gone in the ship. Seeing my musket he examined it attentively for some time, then said, smiling: "White folks know how to pick out good things for themselves." He then showed me his and asked me if they were as good as mine. I told him they were exactly the same—they only wanted cleaning. I offered to clean them for him, and while I was taking the locks apart and putting them together the old man watched me with the keenest interest. When I had finished he said: "Are you a spirit?" I told him no, that I was flesh and blood the same as himself. "Well," said he, "if you are the same as me, what makes you so white?" I told him it was because I belonged to a colder climate and had always worn clothes. But he seemed to think I must have some supernatural aid or I could not take the locks apart and put them together again so readily.

I finished my visit and returned to Labooca to stop awhile with David. I had not been here long before war was declared against one of the villages on the island of Thowcanrover. David and I were invited to join the expedition and messengers were sent to the different villages to warn the inhabitants to appear at the chief town armed and equipped for war early the next morning. When all the warriors were assembled and ready for duty twelve canoes were prepared for the expedition and we embarked for the village of Navarto, where we obtained reinforcements. The next morning a consultation was held as to the best mode, and it was decided to divide our forces, one party to march by land and the other to proceed by water. We soon arrived near the enemy's village, and after going through with the usual ceremony we commenced our march toward the town, and attacked them with arrows. They returned the attack with interest, adding to their arrows showers of stones which seemed to be mostly directed at me. On account of my having clothes on, they apparently selected me for a mark.

CHAPTER VI

I had several hairbreadth escapes from their missiles, but fortunately they were escapes. Eight or ten of us who had muskets marched up, dodging behind trees and stumps until within easy musket shot. David, dressed like a native, led our party. He got shelter behind a stump, singled out one of their chief warriors, fired and shot him through the head. As soon as their chief fell the enemy fled for the woods and mountains. Then we rushed forward, broke down their bamboo fence and entered the village. We killed all who had not made their escape, plundered the town and set it on fire, then marched back to Navarto, singing songs of victory. Here we were paid for our services with hogs, turtles, fishing nets and whales' teeth.

We remained here several days, then embarked for Labooca, where I stopped some time. I next went to Ambow, and there found some of the Raver chiefs who were bound home. Feeling that I should like to see my old chief I took passage with them. The chief at Raver was delighted to see me. He immediately took me to his house and prepared a hearty meal for me. When I had finished he began to question me, asked what I got out of the ship, and why I had not brought my goods with me. I told him I had not got much except a beautiful musket. He examined it very closely and wanted me to change with him, which I did.

I stayed there about a fortnight and was about to return to Ambow, when a messenger arrived from the big island and informed the chief that the enemy was about to attack their town in great numbers, and that unless they received assistance they would have to desert their village. I was sitting beside the chief, who turned to me and said: "Wilama, you go and defend their village?" Though I felt little inclination to do so, I knew that he would be displeased if I refused, so I consented to go. There was one of the Manila men in the house at the time who was eager to go with us, so we made immediate preparations and embarked that evening. On our passage along the shore in a canoe I suffered intolerably from mosquitoes and sand fleas, having absolutely no protection from them, as I was quite naked.

We arrived at the village just before daylight. The enemy were just discernible on the neighboring hills in great numbers. We beat drums to let them know that they were discovered and that we were prepared for them. They continued hovering round the village during the greater part of the day, but made no attack and towards night marched away. Our party then returned to Ambow, where I remained a few days longer, then went to Labooca.

Here I passed the time very agreeably with David. The head chief of Labooca was a very pleasant, agreeable man, but, like all natives, rather inclined to be jealous. When David and I were talking together he was always very inquisitive to know what we were talking about, but we would tell him some plausible story calculated to allay all uneasiness.

By invitation of the chief, we accompanied him to the island of Engow, and while there some of the natives from the mountains saw a vessel steering for the island of Ovalau. They came and reported to the chief. I was of course very anxious to get to her, feeling very certain that it was the Clay, as it was about the time that Capt. Vandaford had agreed to be back (July, 1828). But the wind was blowing a gale and we were unable to leave for two days. At length it moderated and we got underway for Ovalau. We had not been out long before it blew so hard we had to take in both sails (the large canoes always carry a small sail for stormy weather) and steer for the nearest land, which was Butcheak. We anchored there, went on shore, and got some supper. The following day, the weather having moderated, we again started for Ovalau, where we arrived in the forenoon.

On landing, the natives informed us that a ship was at anchor on the opposite side of the island. We (David and I) got a small canoe and started immediately for the ship, which proved to be the Clay. As we neared the vessel, the captain hailed us to know if it was David, and on being answered in the affirmative, immediately invited us on board, and inquired why we had not visited him before. After telling him all the circumstances, he engaged us to assist him in procuring another cargo. He wanted me as interpreter on board and David to assist Mr. Driver on shore. He had concluded not to go to Ambow with the ship, as there were less natives here and he would not be troubled with so many visitors as at Ambow, the distance being so great they would not come off so often. We were about fifteen miles from Ambow. The old chief visited us once in a while, and the captain always made him presents and told me to tell him if he saw anything he wanted to ask for it, which pleased him very much.

Mr. Driver found his beche de mer house in tolerable good order, so that he was soon ready for business and the natives were as ready for trade as ever, but the beche de mer was not so plentiful as on the former occasion. While lying here the captain had a disturbance with his chief officer, put him in irons and turned him out of the cabin. At one time Capt. Vandaford went on a visit to the trading officer on shore, leaving the ship in charge of the third mate, now acting as second mate. On our return next day we found the utmost confusion had prevailed during our absence. The officer had made too free with the liquor and imagined that the boat was cut off and that the natives were about to attack the ship. He had the guns all loaded and was running about the deck like a madman, cursing and abusing everyone. Though nothing serious happened, the captain was careful how he left him in future.

While here, two Ambow chiefs brought off 30 hogs to sell. Capt. Vandaford bought them on condition that they should take them on shore and keep them until he wanted them, when he would pay them two muskets. To this they assented and took them ashore. A few weeks later they returned with them and demanded payment, which the captain refused as the hogs had grown very poor in the meantime. At this they were highly offended. They told him that if he would not pay them what he had agreed he might keep the hogs, so they left them and were about to leave in their canoes when Capt. Vandaford called them back, thinking they might do him some injury in the beche de mer business, and gave them the two muskets, whereupon they departed, well pleased.

After procuring a cargo we prepared for sea. I had now decided to go to Manila in the ship. A few days before we left the king of Ambow came to make his last visit. He expressed regret upon learning that I was going, and wanted I should wait a while longer, but I told him my friends at home were anxious to see me and I must go, though perhaps I might come back again, and that I should never forget his kindness to me. When the old man left us, we honored him with a salute and three cheers. When we were ready for sea we discharged David and the hired men, got under way and proceeded to Myambooa, where we arrived at sunset and anchored. We were visited by the natives and procured a stock of vegetables, etc. The next morning we made sail and before night were clear of all the Feejee reefs and shaped our course for Manila.

Nothing occurred during our passage worthy of special mention. We crossed the line, took the N. E. monsoons, which carried us in sight of the Philippine islands, and the latter part of January entered the straits of St. Bernardino, arriving about the first of February. Our cargo was readily disposed of to the Chinese merchants, who came off to see it weighed, after which the ship's hold was prepared for taking in a cargo of sugar. Capt. Vandaford informed me that he had spoken to the American consul concerning me and that I was at liberty to leave the ship if I chose, or might continue in her until I could do better, and I finally concluded to remain for the present.

We commenced taking in a cargo of sugar, which was brought alongside in lighters. I went on shore on liberty one day and fell in with one of the Manila men who came in the ship. He told me that a Spanish merchant had been talking with him about the islands and that he wanted a man who understood the language of the natives to go in his ship, which he was daily expecting from Canton. I went with this man to the merchant's house, told him my business and got his terms. He offered me forty dollars per month to go as second officer of his ship, but as she had not arrived we could go no farther. He treated me very politely, and I took leave of him with very high opinion. It had been so long since I had been in civilized society other than on ship-board that this merchant's gentlemanly courtesy made a deep impression on my mind.

I returned on board the Clay and informed the captain of the Spanish merchant's offer and offered to continue in the ship if he would give me monthly wages. He offered me low wages, which I accepted rather than go with a crew of half Spanish and Indians. We had about finished loading the Clay, when the brig Quill, of Salem, arrived with orders to take from the Clay such men as liked to return to the islands with an addition to their wages, and to exchange mates. I went on board the Quill to see what wages I could get. The captain offered me fourteen dollars a month, for which I agreed to go, so I took my month's advance to get such articles as I needed and returned to the Clay.

The government here would not permit us to change crews, so the captains agreed to sail in company, and exchange after we got to Angea point. About the middle of March, 1829, we got under way in company with the Quill. We had a very good passage across the China sea until we came to the straits of Gasper. Here we had much light and calm weather. We worked through and on entering the straits of Sunda saw two large prows (a kind of vessel used in the East Indian seas) to windward, heading down for us. A gun was fired from the Clay at them, when they hauled their wind and stood off. We continued our passage through the straits with light winds and pleasant weather. About the latter part of April we came to anchor at Angea point, stopped here two or three days and got some water, and Mr. Driver, with two seamen besides myself, joined the Quill.

Late in the afternoon both vessels got under way and stood out from the land. During the night, the weather being thick and squally, we got foul of the Clay. She struck us on the larboard bow and did us considerable damage. The Clay lost her jibboom, injured her head and stove her quarter boat. Next day we came to an anchor under North Island and repaired damages, then got under way and continued our course through the strait. After passing Java Head we parted company with the Clay.

Nothing worthy of particular notice occurred during the remainder of our passage to the islands. When in sight of the island of Coroo we saw a rankish looking schooner off our bow standing toward us. When near us she luffered by the wind, brailed up foresail and hoisted Chilian colors. Not knowing who or what she was, and as she had rather a suspicious look, we loaded our big guns and prepared for the worst. She kept off from us, came down and spoke us. We found it was the schooner Valador of and from Valparaiso, on a trading cruise among the islands for tortoise-shell, etc. We stood in for the island of Coroo. When we got near the island the natives came off, bringing yams, bread-fruit, etc., for trade. It was now late, so we shortened sail and lay to for the night. At daylight we made sail and arrived at Ovalau late in the afternoon.

We were soon visited by David Whippey and a host of natives who informed me that the old king of Ambow was dead and that he was succeeded by his brother Veserwanker, who was greatly his inferior in every sense. Mr. Driver, the chief officer, was dispatched to Ambow to visit the new king and see if a cargo could be procured. The king thought he could furnish a cargo as well and as quickly as his brother had done for the Clay. The weather being fine we got under way for Ambow, where we soon arrived and were visited by the king and suite. The captain invited the king below and treated him with rum, which he drank very freely and soon found he liked it better than carva. His visits became very frequent and lengthy; he would sit and drink rum until he became boozy; then he would praise the rum saying it was much better than carva and tell me how foolish his head was, which I did not at all doubt, for his actions were quite as foolish as his feelings. When he left us after these visits he would insist on having a couple of bottles to take with him. He used to tell me to tell the captain not to give the rest of the natives any, but to keep it all for him. He was the only one among them that I ever saw drink rum.

We got along slowly with the beche de mer. It was getting scarce and we had frequent spells of bad weather which prevented the natives from going after it.

One day a chief brought a spy glass to Mr. Driver to sell, which he said was found on the reef by some of the natives who were fishing. We could form no idea how it got there, other than that some vessel had been cast away somewhere in the neighborhood. It was nearly a new glass and very little bruised; consequently could not have been long there. Soon afterwards we learned from the natives that a vessel had been cast away on a reef near the Island of Thowcanrover. Capt. Kinsman immediately hired a chief to go in search of the captain and crew. A canoe was prepared and sailed for the island of Somoson. Mr. Page, clerk of the brig, accompanied the chief. On their arrival at this island they found the captain, whose name was Clark, and his mate, some of the crew, and heard of the others on different islands, but could not stop to get them. We found from Capt. Clark that the lost vessel was the same schooner which we had spoken on our arrival at the Islands (the Valador).

The captain said that after leaving us he stood over for the island of Nerg. After trading with the natives he started for Thowcanrover. When near the island he struck on a coral reef. Having lost his boats at the Navigator islands, he had nothing left but two old canoes which were lashed together and with as many as they would carry left the wreck, leaving the crew to shift for themselves. These were afterwards taken off by the natives. They succeeded in reaching the shore in the canoes, but were immediately stripped of everything they had brought with them and threatened with instant death, but were rescued by a friendly chief who heard of the wreck and went immediately to their relief, arriving just in time to save their lives. This chief was always very friendly to the whites. He had frequently told me that if he had known of the loss of the Oeno at the time he would have come and taken us all to his island and protected us. He always protected the whites from assaults and insults. But few are to be found in any country possessed of kinder feelings or more amiable qualities than this old heathen. Capt. Clark said the spy glass was his and came out of the wreck. He and his mate, Mr. Wallis, were kindly received and treated by Capt. Kinsman and his officers and furnished with clothes, of which they were nearly destitute.

It was now the 4th of July, which was celebrated on board our brig by firing big guns and small arms, to the great amusement of the king and natives. They were perfectly astonished at the distance the shot went from the big guns, but did not at all like the noise they made. One day the king, seeing some paint about decks, requested me to ask the captain to give him enough to paint his canoe. He said it would make her look like a vessel. I told the captain if he would give him the paint I would go on shore and put it on for him, which I did, much to his satisfaction. When finished I told him to have a fence built around her to keep the hogs and natives from her, and not to touch her for a week by which time she would be fit to use, all which instructions he strictly followed, and was extremely proud of her, saying there was not another canoe among the islands so handsome.

This old chief was very anxious to buy my fowling piece, but as there was no trading allowed except for the brig I put him off from time to time, but he wouldn't give it up. I finally told him he should have it for the shell of three large tortoises. He went off in pursuit of the shells, which he brought in the evening and took the gun highly pleased with his bargain. The gun having four barrels he thought he should be superior to the other chiefs if he had such an uncommon piece of property.

We lay here a long time, but getting ahead very slowly with our cargo, the Captain concluded to get to Myambooa, as the beche de mer had become very scarce at Ambow. About the middle of October we got under way for Myambooa Bay, where we found the ship Glide, of Salem, Capt. Henry Archer. He informed us that in coming in to the bay he had struck a sunken rock and his ship leaked so badly they had all they could do to keep her free with both pumps. He had heard of a vessel being at Ambow and had sent his second mate in pursuit of her and now began to feel anxious for his safety. Mr. Driver was immediately dispatched in pursuit of the missing officer, and next day both returned.

Preparation was now made for heaving down the Glide. Her guns and stores were taken on board the Quill and some of her cargo was taken on shore at the beche de mer house in care of Mr. Driver who had commenced the beche de mer trade. Having discharged the Glide, a raft was constructed from her spare spars and coconut trees, to which she was hove down, her leak stopped and she was righted again and took in her cargo and stores. We continued our business till December when, having procured a sufficient cargo, we got ready to leave for Manila. When we were about ready for sea Capt. Archer wanted I should join his ship, to which I agreed at thirty dollars per month, and after having settled with Capt. Kinsman, joined the Glide. In a day or two the Quill sailed for Manila.

We now commenced procuring a cargo for the Glide. Having got on board about four hundred picul, and the beche de mer getting scarce, the captain thought it better to shift our quarters to the island of Angalore, where we were told by natives it was very plenty. So Capt. Archer made an agreement with a Myambooa chief to go to Angalore and have a house built before we went with the ship. The chief immediately started in his canoe, accompanied by the chief mate with a plan of the house. In a few days they got a house built one hundred feet long by twenty wide. We then proceeded to Angalore, where we anchored about three-quarters of a mile from the shore. Here the natives brought us the beche de mer as fast as we could take care of it, which enabled us to soon secure our cargo.

It was now the latter part of March, 1830. Having nearly finished our cargo, and being out of hogs and none to be got in this neighborhood, the captain told me I must get some hogs somewhere, so I made a bargain with the chief of Bratter to go to his town, which was about sixty miles from the ship, and get a supply, for which he was to have a keg of powder. A canoe was prepared and I took with me a musket, powder and shot and a few articles for small trade, and started. Soon after leaving the ship the weather became squally and rainy, so we landed at a neighboring village and put up for the night. Having much bad weather, it took us six or seven days to get to the island of Ingaun.

From there I saw a ship lying at anchor at Ovalau, about three miles distant. I immediately procured a small canoe and natives to work her, and started for the ship, but before we arrived it grew dark and rainy, so we landed on the shore at a small village, where I spent a sleepless night, having very sore eyes and surrounded by innumerable mosquitoes. In the morning, after eating a breakfast of boiled yams, I pulled off for the ship, which I found to be the Clay, Capt. Mellitt, from Salem. I informed him who I was, where I was from, and my business, and that the Glide would be ready for sea on my return. He wished me to join his ship, offering me the same wages, but I told him I could not agree to it without the consent of Capt. Archer. After stopping an hour or two and learning as much news as I could remember, he gave me letters for the Glide and I took my leave. Among the letters I found several for myself from home. I cannot describe my feelings on reading these epistles from my sisters nor can they be imagined by anyone who has not been in a similar situation. It was nearly six years since I had heard a word from home.

I returned to the village, where the chief was waiting for me. He was very inquisitive to know what ship it was, who was master, what he was after, etc. We immediately got under way for Bratter, which was six or eight miles distant. On our passage we stopped at a small island, uninhabited, to shoot some birds, which were very plentiful around the shore. The natives told me that this island belonged to the Spirits and if I shot the birds they would be angry and cause some accident to befall us. I, however, paid no regard to their superstitious fears, but shot as many as I wanted. In getting under way again the sail caught so that in hoisting it they tore a large hole. This they regarded as punishment for shooting the Great Spirit's birds. We repaired the sail and steered for Bratter. We soon arrived at the entrance of a small crooked river, took in our sail and poled the canoe up to the town. Here I was detained about a week by bad weather. During this time I visited the Clay, which had got under way from Ovalau and anchored near this place. I spent an evening on board the Clay and returned to Bratter, taking with me a man who had been cast away near the island in a Sydney whaler.

Having collected a hundred hogs and the weather being somewhat better, we started with our hogs in eight canoes. After getting out, the weather grew so bad we landed at Ingram, had a hog baked under ground, and with yams and tarrow we lived well for one day. The weather continued boisterous for two days. It then moderated and we made sail for the ship, which was about fifty miles from us. After running about half our distance the wind blew so strong we struck our big mast and sail and set the small one. The wind still increased until it became so rugged that it was with difficulty that our canoes could be kept free of water. We continued on some time in this way, until the natives were quite exhausted with bailing.

Fearing they would give out and our canoe being old and leaky and heavily loaded, I persuaded the chief to throw the big mast and yard overboard, and told him if that was not sufficient we must heave some hogs over, as the canoe was now half full of water, which was all the time gaining, the other canoes nearly out of sight, and the nearest land twenty miles off. After throwing overboard the mast and yard we managed to get the water out and were enabled to keep her free.

About dark we arrived at the village of Umbawaller. Here we remained for the night. We were now about twenty miles from the ship. Next morning we got under way with a fine breeze and pleasant weather and at night landed on a small island in Wylain bay, about a mile from the ship. There being no huts here we slept on the grass. By daylight next morning we were under way for the ship, where we safely arrived, having been absent twenty days. I was welcomed back with three hearty cheers from the crew, who had given me up for lost. The hogs were taken on board and paid for at the rate of twenty for a musket; the chief received his keg of powder for his services and they all went off well satisfied.

CHAPTER VII

The ship was now ready for sea, and on the 24th of April, 1830, we got under way and steered out, but not being able to find a passage through the main reef before night, put back and anchored at the Island of Anganger. Here we experienced a severe gale, sent down topgallant yards and masts and housed the topmasts. We rode out the gale, which lasted 2 days, without any damage, then got under way and went to Myambooa. We sailed from here the 28th, got clear of the islands and shaped our course for Manila.

Nothing out of the common course occurred during the passage. We entered the strait of St. Bernardino on the 19th of June and arrived at Caveeta on the 25th. After receiving a visit from the health officer Capt. Archer, with a boat's crew, went to Manila. The next morning the boat returned. While lying here the schooner Antarctic of New York, Capt. Morell, arrived, having lost his mate and thirteen seamen, who were killed by the savages. On the 28th we received orders from the captain to come to Manila with the ship, and in the afternoon got under way, ran into Manila roads and came to among the shipping.

After selling the cargo, Capt. Archer concluded to fit out for another voyage to the islands. I was in hopes he would take a cargo for the United States, as I was quite tired of the beche de mer business and was anxious to get home, but in this I was disappointed. Capt. Archer offered to get me a passage to Canton in an American ship which was lying here, so I concluded to take my discharge and take passage to Canton. I accordingly settled with Capt. Archer and took my things on board the Canton ship. I stopped on board of her two days and was informed by her officers that I should probably have to stop in Canton two or three months before there would be an opportunity to go to America. This discouraged me from taking this method to get home, thinking it would about use up what little saving I had made. I then decided I would join the Glide again if I could get fair wages and continue in her till she went. I borrowed the ship's boat and went to Capt. Archer, told him my determination and offered to go with him for twenty dollars per month which, after some hesitation, he agreed to give me.

About the 20th of July, 1830, we sailed for the islands. After getting through the straits we hauled to the northward and crossed the North Pacific Ocean in about the latitude of 30 degrees. During our passage across here, which is called the coast of Japan, we saw a great number of whales and several whale ships. We spoke the ship Zenas Coffin, of Nantucket, Capt. Joy, and two New Bedford ships. We continued our passage for the Sandwich Islands, where we arrived and anchored at the island of Mowee on the 8th of October. Here there were several Nantucket ships and men, and it seemed almost like home to me for a while. Among them was a cousin of mine who could tell me much interesting news from home. The time passed very agreeably. We procured supplies and on the 15th sailed for the Feejees.

Nothing of consequence occurred during our passage until about the middle of November, when we made Perhhyns island, a low island situated in 9 degrees 01' South Latitude and 157 degrees 35' West Longitude. While running along the shore of this island we saw three or four canoes coming towards us. We backed the maintopsail and waited for them. When they got within a short distance of us they set up a terrible shouting and yelling, brandishing their clubs and making all manner of threatening gestures, while still more canoes could be seen coming, but we were well armed and manned and did not fear them. Seeing they were about to surround the ship, the captain ordered a musket fired over their heads as they were crossing the bow, but they paid no regard to it. They came alongside on both sides. We tried to entice them on board, but they would not come. Each one held his spear in his hand ready for use.

Finding there was nothing to be got from them we braced forward the main yard and soon left them astern. They continued following us for some time. Thinking they might come on board, we again backed the maintopsail and let them come alongside. They clambered out of their canoes into the main and mizzen chains still grasping their spears. Capt. Archer turned back-to to them and stooped to take something off the hencoop, when a fellow in the mizzen chains let fly his spear at his head. It grazed his neck hard enough to break the skin. A volley was immediately fired upon them on both sides, and some were run through with boarding pikes. They all jumped or fell overboard. We cut adrift their canoes from alongside, braced full, and left them to pick up their dead and wounded. Some of the crew were anxious to attack them, but Capt. Archer told them there had been too much blood shed already.

This island was nearly covered with coconut trees. The warriors were very dark colored. There were a few women with them who were much lighter colored and had remarkably smooth skins. They had nothing in their canoes except instruments of war consisting of spears, lances and clubs.

Some of them had on necklaces made of hair very neatly braided and where the ends were fastened they had a finger nail secured on.

We continued our course for the Feejees, where we arrived the last of November and commenced business. We had a beche de mer house built on Cambo point, which was about twenty miles from where the ship lay and about three from Ambow village. There being a number of castaway sailors here, they were employed to assist me in curing the beche de mer.

We had not been here long before we had a very severe gale from the N. W. One night I spent in sleepless anxiety, knowing the ship lay much exposed to the wind and sea. I hardly thought it possible for her to ride out the gale. But I was relieved next day from my apprehension by David Whippey, who arrived from the ship. He told me she parted her chain and rode by the hemp cable till the gale was over, when that parted, being nearly chaffed off by the rocks. Having nothing left but a kedge and hawser she drifted in towards the island and came very near getting on the rocks but, getting a favorable flaw of wind from the land, they were enabled to clear the rocks and were then safe but without anchors. They sent to the Island of Somoson and bought the Brig Faun's anchors, for which they gave six muskets. Two boats were sent to me with articles of trade and information that the ship was going to the Island of Mathawater to carry on the beche de mer business and leave me to procure what I could in her absence. In looking over my trade I found there was not enough of some articles and, as the ship was about to leave, I went on board to get what I needed.

When I got on board I found everything in great confusion. The second mate had gone on shore in the morning to cut an anchor stock, when they were attacked by the natives and two men killed, the rest narrowly escaping to their boat. After getting to the boat the officer fired at the natives and killed one. Two boats were then fitted out from the ship well armed and landed, but the natives fled into the woods. The bodies of our two men were taken on board and afterwards decently buried on shore at the village of Labooca.

The captain informed me that the natives were getting to be very troublesome and had made two attempts to take the ship, but their design was discovered in time to prevent it. The first time they came off in canoes, about fifty of them. Some came on one side and some the other. The second mate chanced to look over the side and saw the chains full of clubs and other instruments and told the captain that they were about to attack the ship, when all hands were called to arms. As soon as the natives saw a muster on board they jumped into canoes and went on shore. A few days afterwards they came off again on pretention of selling mats, under which they had their arms concealed, but their scheme was discovered in time to be prepared for them.

Fortunately for us, I brought off a chief with me who wished to visit the ship. When I told him that we had two men killed by the natives of Ovalau he was very much frightened. I told him he need not be frightened, but he was a prisoner for the present. The captain told me to get everything we had on shore off to the ship. We went to Camber with two boats to take off our property. When we arrived we found the men that I left in care of the establishment much alarmed, fearing an attack from the natives. They had been under arms all night. The natives had been very insolent and troublesome during my absence. We immediately commenced loading our boats and five or six canoes which I hired for the purpose.

When the natives found their chief was detained they very readily assisted us to get everything to the boats and behaved very civilly, but I have no doubt if we had not had the chief on board they would have robbed and perhaps killed us all. But they well knew that their chief would have to suffer if they committed any depredations and they valued him more than all we had. We got our boats loaded and made the best of our way for the ship. We got alongside the ship towards night, and when we got everything on board we discharged the canoes and the chief, much to his satisfaction.

About the middle of January, 1831, we left the island of Ovalau for Ambooa, but finding the beche de mer very scarce at Ambooa we went to Angalore. Here we commenced curing the beche de mer. We had obtained about four hundred piculs, when our house caught fire and burned to the ground, consuming about a hundred piculs of the beche de mer. We soon got another house built, but the natives became troublesome, annoying us in every manner possible, both night and day, stealing everything they could get hold of and continually insulting some of our party in the grossest manner, which we dare not resent.

I bore it until it became past endurance and I began to fear that they had still worse intentions. I then went on board the ship and informed the captain of the conduct of the natives and my fears. He went on shore with me and was soon satisfied that it would be imprudent to stop longer and immediately made preparations for leaving. Next morning the boats were sent on shore, into which we put everything of value, set fire to our house, and went on board.

From here we went to Mathawater, where we continued our business till the 20th of March, when a hurricane commenced from E. N. E. We sent down our light spars, housed our topmasts, sent down lower yards and got everything as snug as possible, but about midnight our anchors began to drag and the foremast was cut away, which fell over the starboard side. Directly the mainmast went by the board, taking with it the head of the mizzenmast three or four feet below the top. The ship still continued to drag, but we could do nothing more but resignedly wait the result, being now wholly at the mercy of the wind and sea.

The wind soon shifted to N. W. and blew apparently with double fury. After drifting about seven miles she brought up on a sand spit near the shore. We had on board two chiefs who advised us to stop on board until it moderated and they would see us safe to Mathawater, but the natives began to swim off in considerable numbers, and the captain, fearing they would get to quarreling for plunder and endanger our lives, got his trunk and some few articles into a boat and with a crew went ashore, but were met on landing by a party of natives and plundered of everything.

I remained on board until noon, when our decks and indeed every part of our ship were filled with natives collecting such articles as best suited them. They took all the chests and filled them with their plunder. One chief got about 80 whales' teeth tied up in a blanket and attempted to swim on shore with them. He got a short distance from the ship when they became so heavy he had to let them go, and returned to the ship nearly exhausted in struggling to save his treasure.

All the ship's company being safely landed, save five or six of us, we took the small boat and such articles as we thought we could get off with and left the ship, landing abreast where she lay. We took our things and started for the village of Mathawater, but we had not gotten far from the boat before we were met by a party of natives who robbed us of everything we had and left us to continue our journey. After a very tedious travel of about seven miles we arrived at the village, sore-footed and heartsick enough—at least I was.

We found our beche de mer party at this village had lost their house during the gale and had given themselves up to the natives, who furnished them with another house, treated them with every kindness, and never took any of their property nor molested them in any way. We were also treated with the greatest kindness and furnished by the chief with everything to make us comfortable, but our number being so great we thought we were bearing rather hard upon his hospitality; so seven of us concluded to go to Ambow. We took our small boat and, after four days' passage, arrived at the island of Coroo. Here we learned from the natives that another vessel was cast away at Ambow, but we could not ascertain her name. In a few days we arrived at Ambow and found the wrecked vessel was the brig Niagara, from

Salem. She was driven from her anchors in the gale of the 20th of March. The natives took out the cargo and left her lying on the flats.

After remaining a few weeks at Ambow we went with the natives to Raver to attend a great feast. At the feast they had one thousand hogs cooked and yams and tarrow in proportion. At the close of the grand feast they had a great dance as usual on such occasions. After about two weeks the rest of the crew returned. I preferred stopping here awhile. I lived with a young chief, brother to the king.

Here I remained until the arrival of the barque Perne, of Salem, Capt. Egleston, some time in October. I then went to Ambow, where I met the captain of the Perne at the king's house. I asked him for a passage; he said he did not think he could accommodate me as he already had several more than his complement. I said no more, but next morning I went on board the barque and asked him again for a berth. His answer was, "No, I won't." I turned short upon my heel, got into my canoe and shoved off, when Capt. Archer saw me, called me back and asked why I did not go in the vessel. I told him I had tried to get a berth but was refused and should have to wait for another opportunity. He told me to stop a moment and he would see the captain. After talking with Capt. Egleston he informed me I could go in the barque, so I stepped on board. The same day a schooner belonging to Oahu arrived here, having on board the remainder of the Glide's crew. I remained on board the Perne about three months, when the schooner Charles Dogget, Capt. Driver, of Salem, arrived. Five of us then left the Perne and went on board the schooner. After getting a full cargo of beche de mer among the islands I left her at Raver on the 3rd of April, 1832, when she sailed for Manila.

After remaining here about three months the Perne arrived. I had now made up my mind to leave the island at the first opportunity. The Perne was bound to the island of Rotumah. I thought if I went there I might get a chance on board of some whaler and be enabled to earn something before I went home. A man by the name of William Perkins, who lived with me at the young chief's at Raver, went on board the barque with me to engage passage to Rotumah.

The captain consented to take us, so we went on shore, took a time when the chief had gone on a visit to another village, picked up our things and went on board the Perne, much to the regret of the chief's mother, who wished us to stop until her son's return, but we told her we were only going a short cruise. We left in her care for her son a musket, a keg of powder and a few pounds of lead in hopes it would be some consolation for our leaving.

After stopping here a few days trading for turtle shell, we got under way for the island of Somoson.

In passing Coroo we took on board a white man who left a Sydney whaling schooner. On our arrival at Somoson we found five white men who escaped from Wallis island at the time of the massacre. These men informed me that the natives at Wallis island had taken the ship Oldham, of London, and massacred all hands excepting a small boy, who was saved by an old woman who they believed had supernatural power and could inflict any punishment she thought proper if they disobeyed her. She took the boy and tabooed him and the natives dare not trouble him.

The particulars of the massacre above alluded to were as follows: A man by the name of Minina, of and from Oahu, went there in a schooner with a gang to procure beche de mer, tortoise shell, etc., which he sent to the Sandwich islands by the schooner. He took possession of a small island in the harbor, fortified it and called himself king, but for his arbitrary, oppressive and unjust conduct to the natives they rose and killed his whole crew with the exception of those men of whom I have spoken. The conduct of the captain and crew of the Oldham was as censurable as Minina's. They went on shore and took their women by force and carried them off to their ship, many of them wives, and by many acts of wanton levity and even cruelty the natives became so enraged that they took a time when two boats' crew were on shore, attacked those on board and on shore at the same time, and killed all excepting the boy.

After remaining a few days at Somoson collecting tortoise shell we took on board those Wallis island men and got under way with the intention of going to Wallis island and retake the Oldham. On our arrival there we sent in two boats well armed to reconnoitre. The boats were absent so long we became alarmed for their safety, and fired guns and sent up rockets to hasten their return, which had the desired effect. The reason for their long absence was because the distance from the ship to the shore was much greater than we had supposed. They found that an English man-of-war brig had been there and set fire to the ship and, after losing one man and killing many of the natives, they took the survivor (the boy) and carried him to Port Jackson.

The ship being destroyed and nothing left for us to do here, we proceeded to Rotumah, where we arrived the latter part of July, 1832. Here fourteen of us were discharged who were passengers from the Feejees. I remained here ten weeks, when the whaling schooner New Zealand, Capt. Rapsey, of Sidney, arrived. I went on board and applied for a berth with seven others of our party, but having a full crew and being scant of provisions, we were refused, but afterwards some of his men ran away and among them was his cooper, so I shipped as cooper to receive the same lay that the old cooper had.

We took wood and water and were about to leave when a large whale was seen from masthead, which we took, after getting one boat stove. The weather coming on rugged, we lost part of the head but saved 82 barrels from him. We beat up under the island and landed our stoven boat and the carpenter to repair her. When done, we sailed for the Kingsmill group of islands. Here we spoke ship Milo, Capt. West, of New Bedford, with 808 barrels of oil, and a Sidney barque with many of her crew sick with the scurvey and bound to Rotumah.

We saw a great number of whales around here but only took about 300 barrels. We used up some three months and put away for Rotumah, lacking about ten tons of a full cargo and expecting to get that in our passage. We proceeded to Rotumah, got a supply of wood, water and provisions and sailed for Sydney, where we arrived the last day of December. On our arrival the vessel and cargo was seized, but the crew was paid off for 65 tons, the amount reported.

I stopped in Sydney till the 18th of February, 1833, when I sailed in schooner Clementine belonging to the Isle of France, for New Castle, after coal. We took in at New Castle about 100 tons of coal and returned to Sydney, where we discharged on board of different ships about 60 tons. Then took in a cargo of cedar, barley and cheese, and on the 18th of March sailed for Hobart Town, where we arrived after about 10 days' passage. Here we discharged our cargo and took in a few bags of potatoes and about ten tons of stone ballast and on the 7th of April sailed again for Sydney where, after a very rough, boisterous passage, we arrived on the 23rd of the same month.

After our arrival I continued attached to the schooner for some time. At length the ship Tybee, of Salem, Capt. Mellet, arrived. I immediately went on board, found he wanted men, and engaged a berth. I then got my discharge from the schooner and joined the Tybee. We first took in a lot of hides, horns, hoops and bones. After filling the lower hold with these articles, we filled between decks with New Zealand flax and got ready for sea.

On the 9th of June, 1833, we got under way for the United States, after being searched by the search boat for runaway convicts. We steered out clear of the land, discharged the pilot and steered for New Zealand. On the 16th, fine moderate weather, we passed the Bay of Islands, New Zealand, and continued our course of Cape Horn, having strong winds and fair until near the longitude of the Cape. We then had much light easterly winds with plenty of snow. Went as far South as 63 degrees, where we saw large fields of ice extending to the horizon to the southward of us as far as we could see from masthead. I suffered very much from the cold, having been so long in a warm climate and my wardrobe now not the most abundant. But after a while we got by the Cape, made Staten Island and continued our course for Pernambuco. On our passage spoke an English sloop-of-war from Rio Janeiro for Valparaiso.

We arrived at Pernambuco the 22d of September, got some bread and other supplies, and left for America. We had fine winds and fair weather until in the neighborhood of Bermuda, where spoke schooner Baltimore, from Para. The weather was very squally, with heavy thunder. The schooner which was a short distance from us was struck by lightning, which shivered her mast, then passed down below the deck and went out through her foretopgallant mast, took a piece out of the head of her foreside about six inches above water.

We continued our course homeward. On the 26th of October, 1833, about midnight, we made Cape Cod light. At 9 a. m. took a pilot and about noon came to anchor in Salem harbor.

I got discharged and paid off and took the stage for Boston, where I found a Nantucket vessel in which I engaged a passage. After a few days I arrived at Nantucket, after an absence of nine years. I was received with much joy by my friends and relatives and I believe heartily welcomed by all the inhabitants.

> [1] An article of luxury among the Chinese consisting of
> the dried bodies of Holothuria or sea-cucumber. They
> are found nearly buried in the coral sand, their feathered
> tentacula alone floating above it. Beche de mer is extremely
> gelatinous, and is much used by the Chinese as an
> ingredient in rich soups.